Bargain With A Devil

THE TRAGEDY BEHIND GONE WITH THE WIND

By

Gloria Gravitt Moulder

Cover Design
by
Laura J. Miller

*****

ISBN- 13- 978-0615746517

ISBN-10-0615746519

www.anauthorsart.com

Contents

PROLOGUE

I have always heard that a picture is worth a thousand words, and in this instance I believe it to be true. The death scene photo of Margaret Mitchell made by the Atlanta Police on the cover, and inside this book that shows Margaret Mitchell lying where she fell after my dad hit her tells it's own story.

It shows the ambulance present, and a medic standing looking down at her body, without providing her with medical care, or any emergency effort to transport her to the hospital, inferring she was dead at the scene.

In the photo you will also see my dad with his back turned talking to someone behind him. It shows John Marsh who told everyone he got down in the street cradled, and comforted his wife until the ambulance arrived. The photo shows that to be a lie. He is shown standing behind the gurney talking to a policeman while his wife is lying on her stomach in the position she fell when she was hit, with no one comforting her, or even rendering medical aid.

What happened to Margaret Mitchell has been the most important subject on my mind for twenty years. I attended a meeting recently where there were middle aged, and older retired professional men present. One of them a former coroner. At that meeting I presented a handout of the police photo of Margaret Mitchell's death scene, along with the accident report, and a copy of my dad's indictment, and other documents that are also in this book.

After examining the photo and the documents we proceeded to discuss what was contained in them. The retired coroner spoke up and commented that it was his opinion that he was looking at a dead body in the photo.

It was the opinion of everyone present that if she had been alive that she would have been turned over from her stomach to her back allowing her better access to air where she could breathe. Everyone shared that they thought she was dead.

My dad's thoughts when he was talking to me about it were that she died immediately when he hit her. He said she never moved or made a sound. The medic that came with the ambulance took her vitals then stood up without doing anything to help her.

After she had lain in the street on her stomach for an extensive period of time the ambulance attendant, police, and reporter's stood looking at her,discussing who she was, while the police questioned bystanders about what they had seen.

Dad thought the time line of her death was covered-up by her husband, the police, and others who knew she didn't live five days after he hit her. Her husband had a power of attorney that wouldn't have been valid after her death, making it necessary to keep her alive until her money could be transferred to avoid a long wait while her will was in probate.

The Georgia State Patrol work sheet in the book shows her injury as "fatal" dated on August 12, 1949. Her death wasn't officially declared until August 16,1949. What that means is her death was covered up for five day's by the police, and the powers that be in Atlanta Georgia, whoever they were in August 1949.

After the way my dad was treated by the media and the public I was terrified to do what I'm presently doing. I knew what he told me actually happened to her would be very controversial, and there will be people who will refuse to believe anything except the original story that was mostly lies.

The first thing I did after dad died was to continue the research I had started before he passed away. I also went to the Fulton County Courthouse to get copies of everything they would let me have on my dad's case and that was when I found out about the court sealed file that they wouldn't let me have access to.

I have been back there several times, and they still refuse to open it after sixty-three years. They told me I would have to get an attorney to file paperwork to get it opened, and that it may not happen even then.

This book is not just about Margaret Mitchell and John Marsh, it is also about how the incident that ended her life impacted our family, and made my dad's life a living hell for forty-five years.

I have revised this book from an ebook changed the title and the cover, and added a photo, and some documents. When I published it as an ebook I thought it would be too long, and removed a lot of it. When I decided to revise it, and re-publish it in both an ebook, and a paperback edition, I added back what had been removed.

The documents may be so small you will need a magnifying glass to read them and to look at the drawing on the accident report. I'm sorry about that, but it was the best I could do with the size of the book. I hope you will do whatever you can to enlarge them so you can read them and learn what I am trying to tell you about the lies, and fraudulent charges the State of Georgia used to imprison my dad for ten month's and twenty days.

My purpose for writing it is not for monetary gain or any personal agenda, except to keep the promise I made to my dad. I'm not a literary professional nor do I claim to be proficient in spelling,and grammar. I just have a story to tell and I hope there are people out there that can overlook my lack of writing expertise and look at the historical aspect of the book that tells how Margaret Mitchell actually died from the man who was there. He not only saw what happened to her, he was tried convicted and imprisoned for her death.

DEDICATION

I want to dedicate this book to my dad Hugh Dorsey Gravitt who entrusted me with a secret that he couldn't comfortably talk about for more than four decades.

The secret he told me was devastating to a man whose only crime was to be in the wrong place at the wrong time, becoming the second victim of a senseless criminal act of a killer who needed to brush the cracker crumbs out of his bed, and remove himself from a life he perceived as living like an animal in a cage.

I loved my dad unconditionally, and will love him until I take my last breath. He was not perfect he made the same mistakes most normal people make however; he didn't deserve the hell he went through after the death of Margaret Mitchell the famous author of "Gone With The Wind" when he became the most hated man in Georgia and possibly the whole world.

I was fortunate enough to have him live with me the final three years of his life to share our life stories, where we could be happy, sad. laugh, and cry. Now after many years I can finally tell his story, and keep the promise I made to him before his death.

Rest in peace dad, you deserve it.

LINKED IN HISTORY

The real story behind "Gone with the Wind" was never a love story, it was a disastrous series of events that destroyed the lives of three people, one of them Margaret Mitchell the famous author of Gone With The Wind, the other two were her husband John Marsh, and my father Hugh Dorsey Gravitt.

Margaret Mitchell never met my father however; their names are linked forever in history. The suffering of Hugh Gravitt for forty-five years was not from guilt for her death. It was from the burden of knowing how she died, and that the authorities and the newspapers refused to acknowledge that there was another possible explanation for her, and her husband to be jaywalking, on that fateful day August 11, 1949.

My purpose for writing this book is not to demean or discredit Margaret Mitchell in any way, it is to tell what my father told me about her death that tortured him for for the rest of his life, and made him as much of a victim as she was. She died quickly; his death was slow and agonizing.

He could never come to terms with the fact that no one ever questioned the circumstances of her death. The police, and newspapers who had access to all of the facts in the case, never looked at anyone other than him as her killer.

I will refer to my father Hugh Dorsey Gravitt throughout this book as dad. When I moved to Covington Georgia in 1991 to assist him, his health was failing, and I was worried that he might pass away without us ever having what I would call a close father- daughter relationship, which was something I had wanted my entire life.

When he asked me if I would move there to spend some time with him where we could talk without interruption, and I would be there for him in the event of an emergency, I was divorced, living alone, and between jobs. I had no idea it would be one of the most fulfilling experiences of my life, or that it would lead me to where I am today.

Dad said we have a lot of catching up to do, and we have unfinished business we need to take care of. That statement immediately brought to my mind the incident when Margaret Mitchell was killed that had dominated his life, and impacted mine since it happened in 1949,

As a child, and even after I became an adult I had never been able to spend much quality time with him, he was always working when I visited, and now he was ready for us to sit down together, and talk about the past.

I was not prepared for the revelation I was going to hear, or the effect it would have on me that will stay with me for the rest of my life. What he told me confirmed, and answered many of the question's I had always wondered about the death of Margaret Mitchell.

When he asked for my help I was thrilled. I thought to myself this would give us a chance to discuss things we never had the time for before. My parents divorced when I was five years old, and the separation of our family made it impossible for me to have a close relationship with him as a child. I wanted to get to know him when neither of us had other obligations, and this was the perfect time for both of us.

When I was considering the move, I realized it would help me as much as it would him. I was trying to cope with the death of my twenty-eight year old son Jeff who had a heart-lung transplant on Labor day 1989, and died one month later. Although it had been almost two years since my son died, I was still having trouble accepting that he was gone forever.

I understood how serious dad's health problems were, and knew he might be the next to go therefore; I wanted to be there for him as much as possible. I'm thankful I was given the opportunity to be with him to comfort and help him as much as I could in the final stage of his life.

Prior to 1949, dad was self-confident, with pride in himself, and it showed in his outward behavior. To me he was the best, and I never heard anything that made me feel any differently toward him. My evaluation of him was based entirely on the opinion of my mother, and grandmother along with what I observed, and how he treated me.

I never blamed him for the social unacceptability I felt growing up the daughter of the man the whole world condemned for Margaret Mitchell's death that had a strong effect on my life from the time I was ten years old, that continues to this day, along with a need to set the record straight about the crime committed against her for which my dad was made to take the blame.

What I felt was not shame, because I knew my dad didn't do anything shameful, it took me years to understand that what I felt was the same feeling he had felt for forty-five years that can only be described as being a "social outcast" rejected by society.

I never thought my dad was perfect. He definitely had his faults that were probably more apparent to others than they were to me, although from a different perspective. With all of his personal short-comings I still loved him unconditionally.

After the incident that killed Margaret Mitchell my mother cautioned my sister and me not to tell anyone about our dad's situation. She said people could be cruel when they didn't know the facts in the case, and that it could make those people look down on us. At that age, I didn't understand how something my dad had done could make people blame us.

There were times afterward when I knew what she meant when someone recognized the name, or made ugly remarks about him. It was then that I understood why we seemed so disconnected from the rest of the world.

We found out what she meant when we got to high school and teachers would bring up "Gone With The Wind' and that the author Margaret Mitchell was killed by a drunken taxicab driver that should have received the death penalty. Those instances of teacher ignorance happened to us many times.

THE GRAVITT FAMILY

To explain the kind of man my dad was I have to start from the beginning, and tell how he evolved from being a small town country boy, who after moving to the big city of Atlanta, became the most hated man in Georgia, and possibly the whole world in just five short years.

He was born in "Cumming" a small town in North Georgia on February 6, 1920, the youngest of eleven children, his mother Ada Tate Gravitt was forty-two years old, and his father Robert Lawson Gravitt was fifty years old when he was born.

He had five sisters, Izzie, Bertha, Bessie, Georgia, Lillie, and five brothers, Ezra, Keifer, Egbert, Linton, and Thomas known to everyone as TB. Growing up the baby of the family, with parents who were older he took full advantage of his position, especially with my grandfather who spoiled him, and treated him with fewer restrictions than he had with the older children.

Although my grandfather had other financial interests, they also farmed. All of his brothers and sisters learned early in their childhood that they had to work for the family to survive. Education was secondary; most of their schooling was from the end of the harvest season, until spring planting.

I laughingly asked dad if the purpose of having so many children in that era was to have built in farm workers they didn't have to pay? He said he had never thought of it that way, but it certainly sounded logical. If they hadn't had enough help to do the farm work, many families couldn't have survived.

This was true for most of the farming residents of Forsyth County, who had to dig their living out of the "Red Georgia Clay" from the late 1800s to the early 1950s. Their only alternative was to participate in the making and hauling of moonshine, and if they chose the latter, they still had to grow their own food.

My Grandfather Gravitt kept a close rein on all of them as they were growing up, and he stayed involved in their lives, even after they were adults. I cannot speak for his siblings, but I know that although my grandfather was a strict disciplinarian dad loved, and respected him his entire life.

He told me Ezra was the only one of his siblings he didn't get along with. He thought the reason was that before he was born Ezra was the child who received the special treatment that was later given to him.

Dad said he understood why his brother resented him; however, it didn't make their dislike of each other go away. They never reconciled their differences. When Ezra died, dad didn't attend his funeral.

Some of his siblings were already married with families of their own when he was born. He grew up feeling close to his sisters Bessie, and Georgia who loved and spoiled him, a closeness that lasted as long as they lived.

They treated him, as if he was their own child, and they were very protective of him. He was especially devoted to Bessie and her family, he said they were good christian people, and although he didn't share their religious views, he respected them.

In those days, education was not mandatory in rural communities in Georgia young children had to work sometimes quitting school to help their family survive. People back then considered survival more important than education.

In the early 1930s my grandfather had a small store inside the city limits of Cumming, and when his business dropped off, he decided to make his store business mobile taking it to Atlanta where there was more of a demand for what he had to sell.

Dad helped his father who was in his sixties, start a route in Atlanta peddling fruits, vegetables, eggs, butter, and other items not conveniently available to the people in Atlanta, who became his customers. Today most people cannot even imagine a twelve-year-old boy quitting school to work and help his parents.

Dad said they did very well financially by going to Atlanta with the produce business by adding corn liquor, and brandy for special customers. During the depression, and many years afterward, if you couldn't eat it, or drink it, there wasn't much of a market for it.

My dad was just a boy, too young to drive by our laws and standards today, but his father had taught him to drive as soon as he was tall enough to see over the steering wheel, and reach the pedals, he said it was an exciting experience for him to get to drive the truck in Atlanta, and meet new people, who were very different from the residents of Cumming. It made him feel good that his father would trust him to drive in the big city.

He said the time they spent in Atlanta was a good time in his life. It gave him something to tell his friends back home in Cumming, who had never been there. They were fascinated by the stories he had to tell them about what he was doing, and seeing especially what he saw there, that he had never seen in his hometown.

He told them about how the women in Atlanta wore short dresses, and acted differently from the women he knew in Cumming. He was only twelve years old however; he recognized a lifestyle that didn't exist where he lived that appealed to him, and years later would cause him to lose his family.

He also told his friends about their black customers. Cumming at that time was all white, and it was known as a sundown town, where black people couldn't go after sundown. Those rules were in place for seventy-five years throughout Forsyth County, however there were no such rules in Atlanta.

The people in Forsyth County had removed all black people from the County in 1912, after the brutal rape and murder of a white girl by three black men. Most of the young people who were born after 1912, had not traveled out of the county, and had never seen a black person.

After his father shut down the route in Atlanta, and they went back to business as usual at home, dad had to find something to occupy his time. He was fourteen years old when he started thinking about getting his own car. He had twenty dollars to spend, when one of his friends told him about an old strip down that needed a lot of work to make it run, that he could buy with his twenty dollars.

He knew he couldn't take it home, because he wasn't old enough to own a car, and he knew his father wouldn't allow him to have it. His friend told him if he wanted to buy it he could leave it at his house, and he would help him work on it.

This solved two problems for him; he would have the help he needed to get it going, and a place to park it. This was the first time in his life that he had deliberately defied his father, and he eventually found that there would be unpleasant consequences for his actions.

That old strip down was his first experience doing mechanic work on a car. He knew when he bought it there would have to be a tremendous amount of work done to it before it would run, and he could drive it. With the help of his friends, and their connection to a shade tree mechanic, they learned what parts to buy, and how to fix it.

Finally, after more than a year of trial and error, they got it running, and they felt very proud of themselves for their success, although dad said his conscience was bothering him because he had intentionally done something behind his fathers back that he knew would eventually catch up with him.

He said after all they had to go through working odd jobs to earn money to buy parts and gas, when it was finished they felt relief. Dad said he tried to keep from thinking about what his father would do to him when he found out what he had done without his approval.

Most of the roads in Forsyth County at that time were dirt, and he said he and his friends drove that old piece of a car up and down banks, in and out of ditches, as fast as it would go. As he grew older, he realized how dangerous what they had done with that old strip down had been, and how devastating it could have turned out to be.

He knew it was nothing more than a death trap for young boys looking for "thrills" he said all of them took turns driving it challenging each other to see who could climb the steepest bank without turning over backwards, and who could navigate the deepest ditch without getting stuck.

Just listening to him describe the dangerous things those young boys did with that old stripped down car made "chills' on me just thinking about how much danger they were in.

My grandfather finally found out about it, and made him go with him to the man he bought it from, along with a tongue-lashing he made the man give dad back his twenty dollars, then he gave the car back that was in much better condition than when he sold it to him.

His father didn't ask the man to reimburse dad for the money he had spent repairing it to running condition. He told him that losing the money he had spent on it was his punishment for defying him, going behind his back to buy something he knew he wouldn't allow him to have.

Dad said he was extremely upset because he had invested so much time working on it, and he had spent all of the money he had picked up doing odd jobs here and there. His father didn't take any of that into consideration when he made him return it.

His friend wasn't happy about the situation either. He had spent his time and some money to help with it. Dad said it was probably a good thing that my grandfather found out, and made him get rid of it before he, or one of his friends ended up badly injured, or killed.

More than fifty years later when dad was telling me about it he smiled, and a spark flashed in his eyes, which tells me it was important to him, and a huge disappointment when he lost it, although he knew it was for the best for everyone concerned.

Dad said he remembered things from his childhood that was as clear to him as if it had just happened a few days ago. Things such as driving the truck in Atlanta when he was helping his father and how he felt about his first impression of Atlanta that stayed with him until the people of Atlanta turned on him after the incident that killed Margaret Mitchell.

He got a view of Atlanta that most of the people who lived in Cumming during the depression never saw. Many people who lived in Forsyth County had never been to Atlanta, and probably spent their entire life without ever going there. Dad was very impressed with the big city promising himself he would return there someday to live, although during the depression there wasn't much prosperity anywhere, including Atlanta.

He was in for a huge surprise when he saw Atlanta through the eyes of an adult that was so much different from the way he saw it as a twelve year old child. He soon learned the city he had known as a boy no longer existed for him, and his expectations would never come to fruition.

My Grandfather Gravitt was the most important person in my dad's life, and when he died on November 9, 1949, just a few days before dad went on trial for involuntary manslaughter in the death of Margaret Mitchell he was devastated.

It was a time when he thought nothing worse could happen to him however; something worse did happen, he lost his beloved father, and he was devastated feeling his trouble had hastened his death. It was another traumatic event at a time when he was already under extreme mental pressure, and he didn't know if he could survive it.

The death and funeral of my grandfather added to the trouble dad was in, and it put so much stress on my grandmother that she was unable to attend his trial. She was never the same again after my grandfather died.

He had been everything to her and she just withdrew within herself and got through one day at a time for the next ten years until she died. She lived those last few years in the home of her oldest son Ezra. She died on April 29, 1959. After her death dad rarely went back to Cumming.

MY MOTHER'S FAMILY

My mothers' childhood was very different from dads. The poverty and tragedy she grew up with had a huge impact on her life. My Grandmother Annie Estelle Clark and my Grandfather James Andrew Phillips were married in 1911, when she was fifteen years old.

Although he was a good provider for his family, he was a drinker, and smoker, and she considered them to be bad habits that she didn't approve of. She never went into detail with me about their relationship, but she told me enough that I knew it wasn't an ideal marriage, and after he died, she never had any desire to get married again. She always said once was enough for her.

It was a time when anything happened that involved black people they didn't call the law, they took care of matters themselves taking the law into their own hands.

When I heard the story I'm going to tell you I was shocked that my grandparents personally knew some of the people involved in horrendous acts she was appaled at.

Mama Phillips said that one day during the week in the middle of the day while she was cooking their noon meal there was a knock on the door, and a frantic man from a neighboring farm said his wife had been murdered, and he knew who had killed her.

He said he had hired a black man to help him that day but he hadn't shown up when he got ready to go to the field to work, so he went on ahead. He told his wife that if he showed up later to give him his breakfast, and tell him to hurry that he urgently needed his help.

The noon hour came, and the black man still hadn't shown up so he took his lunch break. When he was approaching the house he could see the back door was open and through the screen he could see his baby sitting on the floor patting in something.

When he walked up to the screen door and looked in what he saw was a horrifying sight, his wife was lying on the floor coverd in stab wounds and blood. She had been raped and killed and the baby was playing in her blood. The man that killed her had also stabbed her many times in the chest with a fork torturing her.

Mama Phillips said the look on the face of that farmer was something she never wanted to see again. It was a look of horrible grief, and murderous rage. He asked her where my grandfather was, and she told him where he was working in the field so that he could easily find him.

The farmer left to go round up some of the other farmer's who lived nearby asking them take their gun and go with him to the home of the black man who was supposed to work for him that day.

When they got to their destination his wife said her husband had left that morning, and had come back later with blood on his clothes, he removed the bloody clothes, and told her to wash them, she refused, then he put them in a tub of water and got in bed telling her if anyone came around looking for him he was sick.

Those farmer's dragged him out of his bed took him to the woods, and hung him up in a tree by his arms with a rope long enough that they could raise and lower him, then they built a fire under his legs where they could burn him, and then raise him up and shoot him in places that wouldn't be fatal.

They repeated that torture until they thought he was near death then they removed his private parts before the husband of the woman he killed took the last shot that killed him.

I asked Mama Phillips what happened to the body, she said she didn't know. She said there were so many lynchings nearby for the rape of white girls, and women that black people were probably afraid to claim the bodies.

She said it was a dark time in Georgia history that she had tried to forget. She said Living in the deep south during the 1920s and 1930s was not easy. She said there were horrible atrocities taking place in that era that were sometimes worse than the great depression.

My grand parents were living on that farm in Vienna Georgia in 1930 when my grandfather died from an overdose of morphine after an attempted suicide, where he had rigged a gun somehow to shoot himself, and ended up shooting one of his arms off.

It was a serious injury that required a daily house call from a doctor who was giving him strong amounts of morphine, Mama Phillips had never seen anyone suffer so much, and she was fearful he would die.

I asked her why he tried to kill himself, and she said she didn't know why, the only thing she knew was that it had traumatized her, and their children. She said his pain was so severe at times that watching, and listening to him suffer was overwhelming for all of them.

My mother was ten years old when her father died. Mama Phillips told me that when the doctor came to make his daily house call she had gone to the barn to milk the cow, and to do the afternoon chores.

Before she left the house she had given my grandfather, his dose of morphine the doctor left with her the day before because his pain level required it be given to him every few hours. It never occurred to her that the doctor would get there and give him an additional dose of morphine while she was out of the house.

She said when she finished her chores and returned to the house the doctor was there, and he had given him an additional dose of the morphine causing her to become frantic when she realized what he had done.

The doctor had warned her from the beginning about the deadly effects of giving him; too much, she had been particularly cautious with it. She told him she had already given him his daily dose of the very potent medication before he arrived, and that she was afraid that what he had given him was too much, but the doctor assured her that what he had given him was not excessive, that he would now be able to "sleep". He was accurate about that, he went to sleep forever.

Later that night after they were in bed with the baby sleeping between them, she woke up to a house that was eerily quiet. When she couldn't hear him breathing, she thought it was strange, because he usually made a lot of noise as he slept.

She reached across the baby, and put her hand over his mouth, and couldn't feel his breath. Panicking, she jumped up lit the kerosene lamp, and started calling out to her children, by the time they got to her she realized her husband was dead.

She had no idea how they would be able to survive without him. She knew she couldn't stay on the farm, because her oldest child was only twelve years old, and it was obvious to her that they couldn't manage all of the work required without the help of her husband. She said all of the children were crying, and she felt helpless, trying to keep them from knowing how serious their situation actually was.

With no phone or any other source of communication, she couldn't do anything until the next morning. She said that gave her time to comfort her children, and to accept the fact that her husband would no longer be there for them, before she contacted anyone about his death. Then she had to get word to his family in Forsyth County that he had passed away.

Mama Phillips said numerous people who knew the circumstances of her husband's death encouraged her to file a lawsuit against the doctor, because he had given him the fatal dose of morphine that caused his death.

She said although she had always wondered why he had given him the extra morphine, without first consulting her about what she had already given him, she said if he asked my grandfather if he had taken any medication before he got there he would have told him no.

She was aware that her husband was telling the doctor how much pain he was in, and begging for more medication saying that what he was giving him wasn't enough to kill the pain he was experiencing, and she thought the doctors' actions were in good faith, and that he didn't kill her husband intentionally.

She didn't have any money to pursue a lawsuit, nor did she know anything about how the law worked in such matters. All she could think about was what she had to deal with every day for her, and the children to survive.

When he died, he left her with five young children to care for alone when she was only thirty-four years old. Donald was her baby and he was two, Dorsey was four, James was six, my mother Murdees was ten, and Wayne was twelve, leaving them penniless during the depression with no means of support.

My grandfather had some kind of falling out with his family that had caused him to pack his family up and move to Vienna Georgia, to a farming community in South Georgia that was about one hundred seventy-five miles from Cumming, and she felt confident his family would not be of any assistance to her after his death.

Her assessment of any help from her in-laws turned out to be accurate they never tried to help her at all however; she said they did bring his body back to Forsyth County for burial relieving her of that financial burden.

She said she didn't know what provoked him to take such drastic steps that he would leave Forsyth County, and never want to move back there. She always knew there was a problem with his family; although he refused discuss what the problem was with her.

Mama Phillips said after her husband died she didn't have a choice except to move back to Forsyth County where she had family who were not thrilled at the prospect of taking them in however; they were the only means of help, and support she and her children had.

When she got to her parents home she was exhausted, and upset after dreading for days what she would encounter when she arrived. Her parents told her they didn't have room for an extra six people in their home, but they did have a "smokehouse" with a dirt floor that she and her children could move into, providing they would do chores and whatever else they could do to pay for the privilege of living in that smokehouse.

Mama Phillips washed clothes, and cleaned house for her parents, and for other people in the community, and Wayne worked wherever he could to get food for them. She told me that many times all they had to eat was bread she fried on the wood heater they used for heat.

She told me she didn't know how they survived, they had to take one day at a time, and do what they needed to do for that day that she could not look toward the future, and she didn't want to remember the past.

She said once when her parents, and brothers were going to kill hogs they needed her help, and promised her a five gallon can of lard to help them, that she was grateful for, she and her children needed it for cooking their food. Several days later she was cleaning house for a neighbor, and when she came back home her lard was gone.

She said it broke her heart to know that someone in her family {she thought it was one of her brothers} would do such a thing when they were practically on starvation however, she was getting use to the fact that anything bad that could happen would find her, and it usually did.

She said when one of her children would be at her parents house doing chores for them at mealtime they would sometimes let them eat with them. On one of those occasions, James was the one they let eat breakfast with them but they would only let him have one piece of sausage and a biscuit, for a growing boy that was not enough, he asked for more, and they refused to give him anything more.

That was just one of the hurts, and mistreatment that she and her children suffered at the hands of her family, and she never got over the way they treated them. She remembered, but she forgave them, and before her mother died, she would go to their home, and help them any way she could. Her father lived into his nineties, living with one of his sons, in his later years.

She forgave them for everything they didn't do for her and her children. I am not sure I could have been that forgiving however; Mama Phillips was a special human being, a much better person than I can ever be.

Wayne had to work, and he couldn't go to school. Mother only went now and then. She said she was ashamed to go because she didn't have decent clothes to wear, and other children would make fun of her. She said after her father died, she never had anything to wear except castoffs people gave her.

She said she was running across the yard when she got home from school one day, when the sole of one of her shoes came loose, her brother wired it together for her so that she wouldn't have to miss school, but she never forgot about having to wear shoes that were wired together that caused her classmates to make fun of her. She finally managed to get to the tenth grade before she had to drop out.

The younger boys went to school sporadically until they became teenagers then they dropped out. I don't think any of them advanced as far as my mother did before she had to give up. All of them led tragic troubled lives. My mother and James were more stable than their other siblings were, although both of them died from alcoholism.

After my mother died, my stepfather called me to come to his home to go through her things, and take what I wanted of her personal belongings, I was shocked at the number of pairs of shoes she owned. She had shoes to match every outfit she had. The shoe incident when she was a young girl caused her to be obsessed with shoes, and clothes for the rest of her life.

Wayne was twelve years old when he had to go out and find jobs at local farms and anywhere else that he could find work to help feed his family. His childhood definitely determined how his life would turn out, when he wasn't in prison which is where he spent most of his life, he had to work at menial jobs because he never went to school where he could learn how to better himself.

Mama Phillips said she thought one of the reasons Wayne turned out the way he did was because he got married to a local girl from the Fagan family when he was eighteen years old, and her parent's didn't think he was good enough for their daughter and made her get the marriage annulled. She said he was never the same after that, and he never got married again.

Most of the work he did for people they paid him with whatever they could give him that his family could use, such as food, and firewood.

When he was in his early fifties he died while incarcerated in a Gwinnett County Georgia Jail where he bled to death from injuries he received from a tractor accident.

Mama Phillips told me she was contacted by an attorney from Gwinnett County who told her the county was negligent in his death, and she needed to file a lawsuit, she never told me whether or not she followed through with it.

She was a person who worried about everything, and took on the responsibility for her family the best way she could, she ended up raising most of her grandchildren for years at a time when their parents for whatever reason couldn't take care of them.

I will remember her, and everything she did to make my life better for as long as I live. I know some of my cousins that she practically raised feel the same way about her. She was special to all of us.

The great depression had started the year before she and her children moved back to Forsyth County. It was a time when the whole country was struggling. I hope no one else had as hard time surviving as Mama Phillips and her children did the years they lived in that smokehouse.

DAD'S FIRST MARRIAGE

In 1938 when dad met my mother Murdees Phillips both of them were eighteen years old, he was young with his whole life ahead of him, when everything seemed to move at a rapid pace. The next thing he knew he had a wife with a baby on the way, and no prospect for a better job in Cumming, or anywhere in Forsyth County.

Work was hard to find in the late 1930s and early 1940s, he couldn't find a job locally, so he joined the Government Funded Work Projects Administration [WPA] and he went to South Carolina to work When I was born on August 5, 1939 my dad wasn't there; he was working in South Carolina. My mother let my Aunt Lillie name me Gloria Ann after the actress Gloria Swanson, and Mama Phillips I have always appreciated the fact that I was named after my grandmother.

A few days after I was born my Grandfather Gravitt gathered several of my aunts and uncles to go see the new baby. All of them got on a school bus one of my uncles was driving and traveled to where my mother was living a few miles south of Cumming.

When my grandfather got back home after the visit, he took some time to think over what the situation for my mother and me was, then he contacted dad's supervisor on the WPA and told him dad was needed back in Georgia, and for him to fire him, and send him home. He did as my grandfather asked, and dad wasn't very happy about it however; there wasn't anything he could do except return home.

His father told him that running off to work in South Carolina when his wife was expecting a baby was not a responsible thing to do, and that he should have known he wouldn't allow him to stay there when he was needed at home.

Many years later when I asked dad why my grandfather was so insistent on him coming home, he told me his father had very strong ideas about the responsibilities of a man with a family. He said he told him he had no business running around the country foot loose and fancy free ignoring his responsibilities at home.

He told him that if he wasn't ready to settle down, he should have thought about that before he got married and started a family. Now he didn't have that choice, he would have to stand up and be a man. It's a shame he didn't put his foot down in that manner when dad decided to move to Atlanta.

I cannot imagine that happening today. Most parents don't have that much influence on their adult children, nor would they dare attempt to force them to follow their guidelines, and rules. When I asked him about it he said, I was smart enough to know he knew a lot more about everything than I did.

Dad told me the next job he had after the WPA was driving a pulpwood truck, which was no easy job, especially when he also had to help load, and unload the truck. He said the job didn't pay much, but it was all he could find in Forsyth County at the time.

They were living with Mama Phillips for a while until they could get a place of their own. As soon as he could afford it he moved us into a small apartment in Cumming. We lived there until he moved us to Atlanta.

My sister Betty was born January 22, 1941, when I was seventeen months old. Dad said, "he felt trapped" he was twenty-one years old with two babies, and his ability to make a living for his family in Forsyth County didn't look promising.

This was the first time in his life when everything looked hope-less. Somehow he always found a way to bounce back. The depression years were a struggle for him, because of the depressed economy in the small city of Cumming and Forsyth County.

The jobs that were available to him were pure back breaking labor, and didn't pay very much, and sometimes he had to accept part time work temporarily until something better came along. It was a time when families couldn't help each other because they were in the same financial crunch, some worse than others.

This was a time when the citizens of Cumming started moving away, where they could find a better life for themselves. His sister's Georgia, and Bessie and his brother TB moved their families to Atlanta where Georgia's husband and TB found work at the Fulton Bag Cotton Mill.

When they would come home for a visit they would talk about how much better their lives were after they moved to Atlanta, encouraging my parents to move there as well. It didn't take much encouragement for dad he was ready to go. He was familiar with the big city, and he was thrilled at the possibility of living there.

For mother it wasn't something she wanted to do. She had to take into consideration what moving that far away from Mama Phillips would mean to her. She had never been more than a few miles away from her, and she didn't like the idea that she would be moving away leaving her widowed mother in Cumming to struggle along on her own without her help.

She knew she would worry about her however; dad insisted they move to Atlanta anyway. Unfortunately for her she agreed to the move, and it was the worst mistake she could have made, their marriage was soon in trouble.

When talking to both mother and dad on different occasions they told me that moving to Atlanta was a huge mistake. That if they had stayed in the country they probably would have stayed together.

I think it would have taken a little longer however; the end result would have been the same.

Floyd and TB told dad if he wanted to move to Atlanta they would help him get a job at the Cotton Mill where they were working. They kept their promise and got him a job. For our family that was the beginning of the end.

I have thought about it over the years, and wondered what was different about my parent's marriage that led them to divorce, when none of the other family members ever went that far. I never figured out what the key ingredient was in their marriage that was different from my parents that kept them together, until death separated them.

We moved to a duplex apartment on Pearl Street in the mill village known as Cabbage Town in Atlanta, and later my mother also got a job at the Fulton Bag Cotton Mill where dad was working, leaving my sister and me in the mill nursery.

Some of my first memories are from that nursery. Betty was a baby, and they would put her down for a nap every afternoon, and made me go outside to the playground where I would sit in a swing and cry until they let me back inside where the baby was.

They would give us a bath every day before we went home. A black woman would scrub me with a brush so hard that it hurt me and made me cry. I begged mother not to leave us there, but she didn't have any other source of child care at that time. To this day the smell of black-eyed peas and cream of wheat cooking reminds me of that nursery.

For the life of me I have never understood what kind of pleasure that woman got from scrubbing me so hard with a stiff brush that I would remember it for all these years.

I also never understood why my parents let her get away with it. I knew the scrubbing hurt me, and I was afraid they would hurt Betty the same way making me afraid to go outside and leave her alone with them. I thought if I was there I could protect her, but of course I couldn't have done any more to protect her than I could for myself.

My parent's marriage was in real trouble by 1943, two years after the move to Atlanta. Dad told me years later that he wasn't ready to be married with the responsibilities of a family at such a young age. He said everything that was off limits in Cumming was wide open, and available in Atlanta.

He said the women he met there were bolder, and different from anyone he ever met back home, and he couldn't resist the temptation to play, therefore, he started seeing other women behind my mothers back.

When I was five I came down with measles causing mother to have to take time off from her job to stay home with me, taking us out of the mill nursery temporarily. When I was over the measles and she was ready to go back to work she decided to hire a friend of hers named Gladys to baby-sit us while she worked instead of taking us back to the nursery where I was so unhappy.

Shortly after we moved to the mill village dad had opened a charge account at the neighborhood store, and he arranged with the man who ran the store to give us candy when we came there without him. He taught me to hold Betty's hand, and look both ways to make sure a car was not coming before we crossed the street.

One Saturday when mother had a day off she let us go to the store to get candy, while we were waiting to cross the street on our way home, lo and behold dad passed with Gladys in the car with him. I ran home as fast as I could, and told mother that I had seen him pass while we were crossing the street, and that our babysitter was with him. He knew I saw them however; when mother didn't confront him about it immediately, he thought she didn't know.

The next week she was working day shift, and dad was working nights. She skipped work and came back home unexpectedly and caught him in bed with Gladys, needless to say sparks flew, and everything she could get her hands on started flying.

My mother who was usually mild mannered turned into a raging mad woman. Dad and Gladys had to run to get away from her until she got over the initial shock of what she had caught him doing. He confessed everything, but mother wouldn't forgive him. That was the last straw for her.

She told him she wanted a divorce. If it had been the first time she caught up with him playing around she might have let it slide. This time she had caught him in the act, and she had no intention of overlooking it.

I can remember her telling about some of his escapades, once when it had been raining for several days he came home after being gone overnight, and she had thrown his clothes out in the mud. Another time she put sugar in the gas tank of his car. When she caught him with the babysitter it was the last straw. That was when she divorced him.

She got a divorce in 1944, and the court awarded her forty-eight dollars a month child support. Dad quit his job at the cotton mill, moved in with Aunt Bessie and her family, and got his first job driving a taxicab for the Yellow Cab Company.

My mother had never liked Atlanta, and she was happy to leave it behind for good. She took me to live with Mama Phillips on a rural farm in Forsyth County where I lived until I was in the second grade.

She took my sister Betty with her to live with her brother James, and his family in Gainesville Georgia. She didn't have a car, and we didn't have a phone making it difficult to communicate with them therefore, we didn't see or hear from them very often.

Dad came to see me at least once a month, when he brought the child support money that was divided between mother and Mama Phillips for as long as I lived there. Most of the time it was late at night after he got off work when I would be asleep. Even though he had to wake me I was always happy to see him.

He never shirked his responsibility to pay child support; he never thought paying it invalidated his responsibility for our needs. He always bought us things on special occasions such as birthdays, and holiday's.

We never went without anything except the privilege of living with him on a daily basis. We didn't get to spend enough time with him to learn very much about him. All I knew was that he was my daddy, and I loved him.

Dad was the first in his family to get a divorce. None of his brothers or sisters followed his example. He was the only one to defy my grandfather, and do the unacceptable.

Many divorces occurred in the families of the grandchildren, and great grandchildren after the 1940s, when it was acceptable to adopt an unconventional lifestyle in which traditional values were no longer the norm.

My parents divorce brought about the worst confrontation dad ever had with my grandfather who was a man who didn't hesitate to tell him what he thought, and where it would lead him. He told him he would live to regret his actions, because his children would have to suffer the consequences of his behavior.

It was the second time dad ever defied his father on anything. The first time was had been when he was a teenager he bought a car and kept it hidden from him while he worked on it.

He knew what his father was telling him about the negative impact divorce nearly always has on children was the right thing to do however; it was too late for him to correct it.

My mother had already filed for divorce, and she would not reconsider. He had been living with that mistake for five years when he hit Margaret Mitchell. After he got out of prison, he went into his own survival mode for the next forty-five years, where his work became the most important thing in his life, and everything else was incidental.

My Grandfather Gravitt didn't approve of dad's behavior after he moved to Atlanta. He realized that he was more than a little wild in his personal life, and the divorce was a result of his disgraceful violation of his marriage vows, he was furious with dad for the fast living anything goes lifestyle he had adopted since moving to the city.

When dad moved away from Cumming his father was very disappointed in him, he told him it would be one of the worst mistakes he could make, and he was right, his whole life started on a downhill spiral after he moved there.

He witnessed, or was involved in one disaster after another between 1944, and the summer of 1949. All of them took their toll on him. It seemed he was destined to suffer dire consequences for his desire to live in the city.

Dad thought he would have access to a better life in Atlanta, but unfortunately it didn't turn out to be true for him; it was the complete opposite of what he expected it to be shattering the dreams of a young boy.

As a man everything good he remembered from his childhood helping his father peddle goods from the country to the residents of Atlanta was different than anything he had experienced before or would ever experience again.

When he went to Atlanta with his father he had to do what he was told to do. When he returned there with his own family his priorities were definately different, although he had the moral support of his brother, and brother-in law he was in charge of his affairs on his own, and he wasn't ready for the new challenges he faced in Atlanta that didn't occur in Cumming.

The difference between the residents of rurual Cumming Georgia, and the city of Atlanta even in the early 1940s was monumental. Dad moved us from a small farming community to the largest city in the south where the bohemian lifestyle was popular, and my grandfather was very upset with him over it.

Most of the people he worked with on his job at the Fulton Bag Cotton Mill had been in Atlanta long enough to adapt to the atomosphere of loose women, booze, and a bohemian lifestyle that was different from the customary traditional lifestyle that most people lived in that era.

A lifestyle dad found appealing and adapted to quickly however; my mother wasn't impressed with the changes, and in order to get her to move to Atlanta he had to convince her that it was the right thing to do, and she was very much opposed to the move, not only because she would have to leave her mother and brother's behind, she wasn't ready to face the unknown challenges ahead, that would change the way they had always lived, and she never really felt at home she referred to Atlanta as hell on earth.

Atlanta was nothing like he remembered it when he was twelve years old, everything had changed, and he didn't know if it was the city or if it was his expectations that were different as he grew into an adult.

The landscape was basically the same, but growing up his outlook on life had changed, he was now responsible for a family that he had to take care of regardless of what he wanted to do on a personal level everything was different for him.

My mother told me that dad changed dramatically after they moved to Atlanta. She said she tried and failed to learn what he liked so much about city life and tried to adjust to the lifestyle that appealed to him, it just never worked for her.

She said at first she tried to talk him into going back home, back to the country where she felt was where they should be that would allow their life to proceed at a slower pace. She could never convince him that was what they needed to do, and as time passed she decided she didn't want him to go back home with her. She was ready to go on with her life without him, and that is what she did.

She went back to the country without him, and the next man she chose to marry unfortunately was worse than what she had with dad.

LIVING WITH MAMA PHILLIPS

I n 1944, when my mother divorced dad, and returned to Forsyth County she left me with Mama Phillips who was living in an upstairs apartment, keeping house, and cooking for Mr. J.P. Elliott whose family and friends called him Jepp. He was an elderly widower who had become ill, and needed someone to live in and take care of him.

Mr. Elliott sent his sister in-law who was Mama Phillips Aunt Flo to tell her about his illness, and that he needed someone to cook and clean for room and board, and a small salary. She had done house cleaning for him before therefore; she wasn't a stranger to him.

Her Aunt Flo Elliott asked her if she was interested in the job. She accepted the offer, and kept that job until he died in 1956, when he was in his eighties.

When he recovered from his illness, she continued her job in his home doing the same things she had done from the beginning, except he was no longer bedridden, and he regained his health quickly under her care, making sure, he took his medicine, and ate right.

I think he would have been lost without her if she had moved on after his recovery. They had become good friends who could, and did communicate with each other in a fashion that I think is key to any friendship, and I know for a fact there was never anything more than that between them. The salary he paid her was two dollars and fifty cents a week.

That seems incredible today, but he saw to it that she never wanted for anything as long as he lived. She used the small salary he paid her for coffee and tea, and the other little extra things she wanted from the peddler she called the coffee man.

Everything else she used barter to buy what she needed from Pendleys store on highway 19, about two miles from where we lived. She didn't need money she used eggs, and butter. During the depression sugar was rationed, and she got coupons in the mail to pay for that.

Before Mr. Elliott died he gave her some money, I don't know the amount, but it saw her through the hard times after his death. It was a very sad time for us when he died. Mama Phillips and I knew we had lost something important in our life, and that was our best friend. Someone to tell us stories, who could make us laugh, and talk to us about things important to us.

He could always make us see beyond the negative, and appreciate the life we had. His death was a sad time for us. He has been dead for more than fifty years, and I still miss him, and his wisdom.

The time I lived with Mama Phillips in Mr. Elliott's home after my parents divorce I was happy. I loved that old man as if he were my grandfather. He was a kind and generous man who had seen sorrow when his daughter died as a young child, and when he lost his beloved wife Jenny that, he adored.

He had a large old trunk that contained items that had belonged to his wife and daughter, and at times when he was missing them, he would open it and pick up things that they had treasured, and hold them. Mama Phillips told me not to disturb him when he was doing this, that we needed to respect his privacy.

He would tell us about their life together, and he said they hardly ever argued that if he ever felt anger he would go outside until he was over it. He said they never went to sleep angry or mad in all of the years they were together.

I slept with Mama Phillips in an antique bed with a featherbed on it that was like sleeping on a cloud. I have never slept on a bed that comfortable since.

In the winter for foot warmers, she would put the black irons she used to iron clothes on the hearth in front of the fire. When they would get hot enough, and we were, ready to go to bed she would wrap them in a blanket, then put them in the bed for us to put our feet against to keep us warm.

She would get up before daylight every morning after Mr. Elliott had built a fire in the wood cook stove, and they would cook breakfast together. I will never forget that time in my life. These are treasured memories from my early childhood that are very special to me.

When breakfast was ready she would wake me, and the smell of coffee brewing, and ham frying was wonderful. After breakfast, the daily chores would begin, and while Mama Phillips milked the cow, Mr. Elliott would go into the corn crib and shell corn for the hogs, and chickens.

While they were doing the chores, I would explore the barn loft looking for eggs where the hens would sometimes get up there and make a nest in the hay.

One morning I found a nest that was full of eggs, not knowing any better I pulled the hem of my dress up and made a place for them. Then I tried to climb down out of the barn loft with the eggs that had been there so long they were rotten, and of course, it was impossible for me to get down without breaking them.

The odor of rotten eggs was horrible, and I got it all over me, needless to say it took a good scrubbing to get me, and my clothes clean and odor free.

Mama Phillips and Mr. Elliott thought it was funny; however, I didn't think there was anything funny about the horrible smell and the embarrassment of not knowing better than to try to get down out of the barn loft with rotten eggs.

I would avoid the corn crib where Mr. Elliott kept a black snake to keep down rats. I saw it a few times, but I kept my distance, although child like, it never occurred to me that the snake could have been anywhere in the barn, that it was not confined to the corn crib.

I have always been terrified of snakes, that are plentiful in Georgia and to me there is no such thing as a good one however, he insisted there was a good reason to have it. He said there would definitely be rats eating up his corn if he didn't have the snake, and that it would leave if it didn't find food in the barn.

Mr. Elliott's house was two stories with two porches on the front that ran the width of the house. My sister and I played on the second floor porch with our table and chairs we received for Christmas, where we had pretend tea parties with water and raw peanuts. Sometimes in the summer, we would move everything outside under the huge oak trees in the yard.

Mr. Elliott had a large fruit orchard, with several different kinds of peaches, apples, pears, figs. Grapes, cherries, and a huge black walnut tree in the back yard that provided us with all the fruit and nuts we wanted. Making ice cream with a hand crank ice cream freezer under the walnut tree in the summer was a real treat for all of us.

The house was large and there was always something to do. Mama Phillips was an immaculate housekeeper, and stayed busy with one thing or another all the time. She was never afraid of work. I never saw her just sitting around doing nothing. She ironed everything, with black irons she heated on the stove; she even ironed the flat sheets, and pillowcases.

I don't remember her ever having a broom purchased from a store while I lived with her. However, that doesn't mean she didn't sweep the floors. The straw brooms she made performed quite well. We would go up on the hill behind the house, and cut broom sage, and bring all we could carry back to the house.

She would choose the size she wanted her broom to be, then secure it with rubber strips, and wind it turning it until she got it down as far as it needed to be to make a broom, then she would take a fork and get all of the loose particles, and seed out of it. She would make three or four at a time, enough to last her for a year.

Every spring we would go down in the pasture to a small stream where we would get what she called white wash that looked like gray mud when we got it, but when it dried it was white, we would use it on all of the fireplaces to make them as white as if we had used paint.

Mr. Elliott operated a cotton gin three days a week, and when he wasn't working at the gin, he worked in his blacksmith shop shoeing horses, and repairing farm equipment that kept him busy. I was fascinated with the work he did in that blacksmith shop.

I don't remember ever hearing Mama Phillips complain about anything, and I know she had many sorrows and unhappy events that she had to address however; she handled them privately. We always had what we needed, and there was never any bickering or arguing.

I was too young to realize at the time that people all over the country were struggling to survive. I thought we were rich, and that everyone had the same things we had. That was the only time in my childhood after mother and dad got a divorce that I lived in a peaceful home.

One of my favorite memories from living at Mr. Elliott's home was riding in the rumble seat of his "A model car he called jacklegs". He didn't drive jacklegs very often, but he would sometimes take us for Sunday afternoon rides in the countryside around Cumming, and at all other times he kept it in a locked shed, where no one except him had access to it.

The only other means of transportation we had at first was two mules and a wagon, and a two-ton work truck that belonged to his brother Joe Elliott who owned the cotton gin that Mr. Elliott operated for him, and later he bought a pick-up truck that he drove until his death.

The only time we didn't have access to the entire house was when Mr. Elliott's children came to visit, and that wasn't very often. When they were there, Mama Phillips would take me upstairs to her apartment until they left.

The only negative memories of the time I lived at Mr. Elliott's home was at election time when men who were running for public office would come to visit and bring Mr. Elliott peach brandy that they would drink, then they would take him to Cumming to vote.

I never understood if he voted for them because they were the right candidate for the job, or was it because they bought his vote with peach brandy, and fast talk. I was a young child, but I realized what they were doing was wrong. I remember that and wonder how politicians are bribing their constituents today to get their votes.

We didn't know what television was back then, all we had was a radio, and Mr. Elliott always wanted everything quiet when he listened to the news. We would sit quietly and listen although I didn't know what it was all about; I knew that at times something serious was happening that involved war, and the United States.

Every evening after we ate, and finished with the chores we gathered around Mr. Elliott and got ready for exciting ghost tales and stories from the past. This is one of my favorite memories listening to Mr. Elliott and Mama Phillips tell those stories.

He knew a lot of the history of Forsyth County, and the surrounding area, and Mama Phillips would tell us about the years she lived in Vienna Georgia. Those stories fascinated me, although some of them were of a violent racial nature they made an impression on me that I remember all these years later.

One of the stories Mr. Elliott told was about the rape and murder of a young Forsyth County girl by the name of Mae Crowe by three black men. The rape was so horrible that the whole community was outraged. They had one of the black men locked up in Cumming when a large group of local men stormed the jail, and killed the prisoner.

He said that after the man was dead they tied his body to a wagon, and dragged him around the courthouse square until his legs were just strings, then they hung him on a pole where the public could see the consequences of what happens to black men who rape, and kill white girls.

Later they went to the home of every black family in the county and gave them an ultimatum to leave Forsyth County or face the consequences. They removed more than a thousand black people from Forsyth County in 1912, and for seventy-five years, there were no known black people living there.

Mr. Elliott pointed out some of the houses on highway 19 in Forsyth County where black people had lived that still had bullet holes around the front doors where they were threatened, and forced to leave the county.

The fear felt by those black people who had nothing to do with the murder and rape of the Crowe girl had to be horrendous. I believe in punishment for the guilty, but holding citizens of the county responsible for the actions of others, because of their race was wrong.

Those people some of them owned farms, and homes, and had done nothing to deserve it lost everything they had, all because of the actions of the three men who committed a horrible crime that no punishment they could have received would have been enough regardless of their race.

When I was growing up, I heard the Mae Crowe story, as well as many other brutal incidents that fired up the community to the point of their refusal to let blacks live anywhere in the county, or even pass through after sundown for many years. I suspect the old timers who still live there are telling that story to their children and grandchildren to this day.

The bad memories will linger forever in some peoples mind. Things are different in Forsyth County than they were when I was growing up. The signs at the county line telling black people not to let the sun go down on them in Forsyth County that were there for many years are gone. On the surface, there are no racial issues, people of all races can live in harmony in Forsyth County.

Marriage from Hell

My mothers' life was chaos from the time she was ten years old until she died, caused from her fathers' suicide, and growing up in poverty as a result of his actions, and her short marriage to my dad that ended in divorce, and her second marriage that was even more of a disaster from the beginning.

She married Ralph Phillips [no relation to our Phillips family] in 1946. That marriage lasted until her death December 7, 1971 at the age of fifty-one. Her life was short because she chose to live in misery with an evil man, whose lifestyle had encouraged her to abuse alcohol.

She died a horrible death from cirrhosis of the liver, brought on by the heavy drinking she had done for more than twenty-five years. Ralph always had liquor in the house, she would drink with him every day, and after a few years, she said she had to drink to stand the abuse she was getting from him.

To me that was just an excuse not to leave him, and try to make a better life for herself, and for us. I would beg her to leave him. I would try to convince her she could make it without him, but she would never leave him for more than a few days at a time. I was so ashamed of the way we had to live.

I always felt our lives were so explosive all the time because of Ralph's lifestyle that we had to deal with. We rarely had friends come to our house, because we didn't want to get embarrassed.

When my mother first married him he told people he was a farmer, and he did make an effort to farm, and raise chickens. However, most of the money he made those years came from gambling, and running moonshine from the North Georgia Mountains.

The lifestyle Ralph made us live for many years was unacceptable to me. I hated it. The drinking, hauling moonshine and gambling was definitely not a lifestyle I could ever be proud of, or would have ever chosen for myself. I was just a child, and I didn't have a choice.

I only remember a few times when he would have his gambling friends come to our house to play poker or whatever game of cards they could gamble on. At those times when they were there we had to stay outside.

He never let them come there when mother was at home. If they happened to be there when she came in from work they would leave immediately. I guess they knew she didn't approve of what they were doing.

Many times, he would take us with him to the mountains, and to Dawson County to buy corn liquor, he rarely let us get out of the car, nevertheless we knew why we were there. We knew who many of the bootleggers were in the County. It wouldn't have been obvious to strangers what they did for a living they were just ordinary people trying to make it in hard times.

We would go through the middle of Cumming with the car loaded with moonshine, and never have a problem. The only law enforcement bootleggers and liquor runners had to worry about in Forsyth County at that time was federal agents.

The local law enforcement knew who was running, and selling moonshine, and looked the other way, this was common knowledge in the county. Most of the bootlegger's were well known by everyone.

When dad and I were talking years later I told him about Ralph, and his supplementary source of income. He said he never had a clue Ralph was hauling moonshine, especially that he was doing it with us in the car. He said he knew he was a heavy drinker, but he never suspected what was really happening in our home.

Ralph would buy us candy and soft drinks on those trips, and we enjoyed that. We never considered what would happen to us if the police were to stop him. No one ever asked us anything about it, and we instinctively knew to keep our mouth shut about what we were seeing.

He was the first boyfriend mother ever had. She dated him before she met dad. When he returned home after two years in the army, she was divorced, and they got together again. Mama Phillips despised Ralph, and didn't want mother to have anything to do with him, but she couldn't stop her from seeing him.

Mama Phillips always liked dad, and he liked her, even though he and mother had their problems, she never put all the blame on him. Ralph was a violent man who didn't talk much, and she never trusted him. I think her dislike of him influenced my opinion of him to some degree.

Ralph's father Marshall Phillips was a bootlegger in Forsyth County, a very domineering man. I think his son was a lot like him. His mother was one of those women who never believed her beloved son would do anything wrong however; she was definately opposed to Ralph marrying a woman with a ready made family.

I remember times when his mother and my mother would argue and she would say something about Ralph having to raise children that were not his, and my mother would tell her that he knew she had us when he married her, and there wasn't anything she or anyone else could do about it, that we were there to stay.

One Saturday before they got married he had a date with my mother, and his father insisted Ralph take him to Dawson County to buy what he called "white lightening". It took longer than he thought it would, and he was running late for his date.

By the time, they got the car loaded, and left the bootleggers place Ralph was mad, and driving too fast on a crooked dirt road, his dad kept begging him to slow down making him mad causing him to drive even faster.

The car Ralph was driving had a feature that when the switch was turned off it locked the steering wheel, either his dad didn't know that, or he was too scared to remember it. When Ralph kept refusing to slow down his dad reached over and turned off the switch.

Ralph using every bit of strength he had, he couldn't prevent the car from leaving the road and crashing. Marshall Phillips died in the accident, and Ralph had a broken arm, and other less serious injuries.

The wreck happened close enough to the house where they had purchased the liquor that Ralph was able to walk back and get help. When the bootlegger realized Marshall Phillips was dead, and Ralph was hurt he knew they had to work quickly to clean up any evidence that the liquor was in the car.

Since the accident happened several miles out in the country in Dawson County, they knew they had time to take care of the situation before they contacted law enforcement.

They were way ahead of Ralph when he told them to get the liquor out of his car, and do something with it before the sheriff got there. They were well aware of what they had to do. Some of the glass jars had been broken, and the smell of liquor was strong.

He didn't go into detail about how they went about the cleanup, but I suspect the man who had sold them the liquor as most of the people in that business would have had ways around a serious situation like this; after all, it was in Dawson County where corn liquor was a major source of income.

They loaded the liquor that had survived, along with the broken jars into their pick-up truck, and hauled it away before they called to report the accident. Ralph always said they were very good at cleaning up mishap's.

When the sheriff, and the ambulance got to the scene all they saw was a wreck with one man injured, and one dead. There were no charges filed against Ralph for his fathers' death it was ruled an accident.

However, the guilt he felt was overwhelming for him at times, and I think it may have contributed to his violence against my mother. I know his father's death was part of the problem, and when he was drinking, he would blame her.

He would get mad at her and say, if he had not been in such a hurry because he was going to be late for his date with her his father might still be alive. He was very good at shifting the blame for his wrongdoing on her.

The first house he moved us into after he married my mother in 1946 had electric lights, and running water, however; it didn't have an inside bathroom. Dad bought us our first bicycles for Christmas that year, and we had to learn to ride them. I will never forget that experience, it was awful.

Our driveway was sloped, and mother would get at the top and turn us loose, and Ralph would get at the bottom to catch us, and that didn't work for me. I feared him and despised him at the same time making it impossible for me to concentrate on learning anything. Pretty strong emotions for a young child trying to learn to ride a bicycle.

When I would get my bike going fast enough to keep it upright I would look up and see him then fall. I was falling so much mother was afraid I was going to get seriously hurt she told me to put my bike away until later. They finally left me alone to learn on my own, when Ralph wasn't around.

My sister learned to ride before I did, she wasn't afraid of Ralph therefore, making their effort to teach her to ride worked for her. I never got over my dislike or fear of him as long as I had to live in his house. After I became an adult, and he couldn't tell me what to do any more I just tolerated him.

Dad was always buying us things, never missing birthdays, and holidays such as Christmas, Valentine day, and Easter bringing us the gifts after he got off work a few days before the occasion. He was never there with us at those special times, but he always made sure we received most of the things other children who lived with both parents had.

I remember thinking I would rather spend time with him than to get the gifts, although I appreciated, getting things from him that mother couldn't afford to buy us. I knew he had a busy work schedule working seven days a week; he didn't get off very often on weekends or holidays.

He would explain to us that he had to work long hours in order to survive himself, pay child support, and buy us the things we wanted., and that made sense to me, although I loved him, and wanted to see him as often as possible I had to accept his situation.

I always considered him a special part of my life, although I knew I couldn't live with him, I just accepted that was how things were, and I didn't question it further. I always dreamed there would come a day that I could live with him.

After my mother married Ralph we moved often. We only lived at that first house for about six months, and then Ralph moved us to a large farm known in the community as the Old Russ Place.

Although I don't know how many acres were there, I know it covered a large area. With chicken houses, storage buildings, a large barn, and a non-working syrup mill.

It was on a dirt road in a remote area of Forsyth County and this was my first experience with hard work, and real fear, it was an isolated wild, and snake infested place.

To keep a farm that large running it would take several adult men, Ralph only had the help of mother, my sister, and me, and occasionally some of his relatives that traded work with him.

When we moved to that farm I had never been made to work, and I wouldn't have believed it if anyone had told me how my life was about to change. I would learn to get out of bed before daylight, and work hard all day. He told us if we were going to live in his house we would earn our way, and he made sure we did just that.

When dad and I first started talking about the past, I asked him if he remembered that farm. He said he did, and he said Ralph had told him how hard he had to work to help support us, and that we were too lazy to help him.

I said dad, if we had been too lazy to work, it wouldn't have made a difference to him. It was not a matter of choice. He never asked us if we wanted to, it was mandatory or he would beat the daylights out of us, and that included our mother if we disobeyed him.

I asked dad if he believed what Ralph said about us, and he said he didn't know what to believe because at that time I had never told him how Ralph was treating us, I was afraid of what he would do if he knew.

Dad said he didn't think much about the fact that we didn't have modern facilities; many of the people living in North Georgia in that era lived that way. He said very few of them had running water, electric lights, or inside plumbing, many of them were worse off financially than we were.

I told him I might have been blaming Ralph for the hardships we had to live with when it was just the times. That may have been partially true, but hard times didn't cause the abuse. There was never any doubt in my mind where it came from, or why.

I was eight years old, and Betty was six. This was her first year in school. We had to walk a quarter of a mile to catch the school bus leaving our house before daylight in freezing weather. I can remember how frightened and cold we were when we would hear wild animals, or when we heard dogs, and thought they were after us.

We also had a neighbor we didn't trust. He would ride by our house on his horse at the same time we were walking to meet the school bus. That neighbor owned a diary farm about three miles from us.

He was a scary looking individual, and we were terrified of him. He had a beard that prevented us from seeing anything except his eyes and nose, and seeing him in that light made him look even scarier, although he was probably harmless, he certainly didn't look harmless to us.

Rumor in the community was that he had a wife and at least one son who lived with him. I don't know if that was true, we never saw anyone except him. There were also rumors that he had gone to Gainesville Georgia, got two black men, and a black woman out of jail, and brought them to his diary farm to work.

We never saw them, but we did see the cross-burned by the KKK after they learned the black people were living in the community. They ordered him to get them out of the county, and if he didn't comply with their warning, they would be back and it would be too late, that they would hang the black people, and burn his place to the ground.

I don't know if he took those people back where they came from, or if something sinister happened to them. As long as we lived there, we never saw any more signs of crosses burned, and no one came around asking questions about them.

The neighbor continued to ride his spotted horse by our house at dusky dark, and sometimes before daylight. He never seemed to pay attention to us, and we never knew where he was going. We thought he was just ridung his horse to exercise it, and for pleasure.

There were four chicken houses on the farm where we lived, that held about eight thousand chickens, which was a small operation by today's standards. When you consider that we had to fill each feeder by hand, and the only water was well water that we had to draw from the well, and pour into barrels, it was a massive job for a small family.

Sometimes when his work was finished, and he didn't have work to do at home, Ralph would help his brother in-law with his farm work, and then the brother in-law would return the favor when he could. If his crops were ready before ours were, we would help him, and he would bring his children to help us when ours was ready.

I can remember drawing water when I was eight years old until my arms would feel like they would fall off and my nose would bleed. I could only stop long enough to get something to try to stop the bleeding.

My mother apologized to me for what I was being made to do and in the same breath saying she and Ralph couldn't do "everything" that they needed my help. I never complained about anything to dad when he came to visit. I never thought there was anything he could do to help me.

On that farm we had cows, and hogs, as well as the chickens we kept for eggs. We also grew cotton, corn, and vegetables that would have been back breaking work for an adult, and it was worse for little girl's who were made to work from daylight, until dusky dark during the summer, and after school during the months we were in school.

We didn't even try to avoid the work because he watched our every move and if we ever started slacking he would tell us to get back to work or he would take care of us later, and we knew that meant a peach tree switch with stripes all over our body that would last for a very long time.

We didn't have modern equipment to do the work for us, we had to do everything the hard way. Sometimes we would get big rats in the chicken houses that would kill large numbers of chickens during the night that would cause Ralph to sit in the chicken house all night with his gun and shoot rats as large as a small cat. I have seen him kill four in one night.

We never had time to play, and do things other children could do. Ralph's sister and brothers didn't make their children work the way Ralph made us work.

They were the only examples we had to go by, because we never had access to anyone else our age, except at school, and we didn't discuss such matters there. My mother couldn't help us with this or anything else, she didn't dare confront him about anything.

At that time it was just hard work to me although I now realize those years we lived on that farm taught me how to work. It also taught me some good lessons of survival that I think the younger generation is lacking today. As hard as farm life is, it has always been my preference of lifestyle.

When we were out of school, we were up before daylight, sometimes went to bed before dark after we ate, cleaned up the kitchen,
and got our bath in the #2 galvanized wash tubs we filled with water
in the morning, and left in the sun all day to heat. By that time, we
were too tired to stay up longer.

Once after Ralph sold chickens, and had money to gamble with,
he left early in the morning after giving mother orders for what we
were to do while he was gone. She knew he was going to play poker
with his gambling friends, and would possibly come back with no
money, and take his frustrations out on her.

She usually did what he told her to do, but this particular time
she ignored his orders, and did what she wanted to do for a change.
When he came home he was drunk, and she was lying across the bed
reading a True Story Magazine instead of going to the field to chop
cotton as he had told her to do.

We always knew when his luck had been bad gambling because
he would be violent with my mother afterward, he knew she would
tell him what she thought about him gambling away the hard-earned
money we had helped earn.

when he came in, he began cursing her, and grabbed her by her
feet and slammed her head into the wall, terrified I ran into the
kitchen looking for something to hit him with to take his attention
away from what he was doing to my mother. All I could find was a
stick of wood used for the wood cook stove, I grabbed it and threw it
at him, and that just infuriated him more.

There wasn't any way for me to help my mother when he hit her and left bruises all over her body. Although I was only eight years old, I always tried to help her, and sometimes I could draw his attention off of her, while he beat the daylights out of me.

Mother always said the reason he lost playing poker was that he would get drunk, and the other men he was playing with would take advantage of him, and take his money. She said when he stayed sober he usually won.

After two years of trying to survive on the farm Ralph decided it was never going to be a successful venture. A man with only two young girls and a woman couldn't do all of the backbreaking work it would have taken to make that farm profitable.

We moved again this time to a small house next door to a bootlegger, and he started hauling moonshine from the mountains. Moving was something we had done on a regular basis since mother married him.

Dad didn't know he was gambling, and running moonshine on the side. He said he never discussed anything with Ralph about how he made a living. He never wanted to pry into his business, although he told me years later that he should have made it his business, after all, we were his children, and we were living there.

I told him about Ralph coming in from one of his gambling binges, and putting a huge stack of money on the table, then he told us he would give us ten dollars each if we could count it, of course we got too excited at the site of all that money to count it accurately therefore; we didn't get the ten dollars.

He frequently won several thousand dollars when he was on a winning streak, when he lost, which he often did, he would turn into a drunken monster that we would have to run, and hide from. Our lives felt like we were on a roller coaster for years. Sometimes up, more often down.

He would find something to confront mother with to start a fight, then we would have to run from him, leaving the house in fear, then he would lock us out of the house until the next morning.

We would hide behind the chicken house, or the barn, until he woke up sober, and unlocked the door to let mother inside to cook his breakfast. Mother would never go to the neighbors for help; she didn't want them to know what was happening in our home.

After one of those episodes, she would cook his favorite breakfast trying to please him. He liked what he called cathead biscuits, and sawmill gravy, with the sausage she had canned in pint jars when we killed hogs, making his favorite food, she was hoping he wouldn't continue the violence from the night before, although she knew it would just be a matter of time before it happened again.

The Christmas after I turned twelve Ralph had won a substantial amount of money gambling, and he bought mother the latest luxury model electric stove, and a large doll for Betty.

He explained to me that he was giving the doll to her because she was the baby. He didn't give me anything, although dad, and Mama Phillips didn't forget me, I never forgot, nor did I ever forgive him for slighting me.

I could never understand why my mother put up with him, and his lifestyle. I hated the way he treated me however I was helpless to do anything about it without making matters worse for all of us.

Dad asked me if I knew why Ralph always wanted mother to work outside the home. I explained that prior to him getting a job at the Coca Cola Company in Atlanta in the 1950s where he worked until he retired after twenty years.

I don't remember him ever having a job where he brought home a paycheck, before then most of his money was made from gambling, and hauling moonshine to the local bootleggers.

It was a fact that someone in the home had to work, and mother was the one who went to Atlanta and got a job. The child support money wouldn't cover everything, even though the cost of living was much less in the 1950s.

She didn't have a car therefore, to work in Atlanta she had to find someone in the community who also worked near enough to her job that she could ride back and forth to Atlanta for a fee. That was a routine she kept for years, leaving home very early in the morning, and getting home late in the evening.

He made her work until she had to quit because of health issues just a few years before she died, when she wasn't able to work any longer. Dad said she never discussed her personal life with him after she got married again however; while she worked in Atlanta she would call him regularly keeping him up to date on how we were doing.

Ralph made sure she kept a job as long as she was able to work but he never let her have anything in her name, not even a bank account, he would take her paycheck and deposit it into his account, and her name was never on any property he owned. She completely lost her identity after she married him she became invisible.

I remember one farm, and other homes he owned all in his name only. He did buy a car once, and told her it was hers, but the title was in his name, and she could only drive it with his permission. He treated her as if she was his slave, and she didn't have any rights.

I fought all of it until I finally had to give up because she wouldn't defend herself against him. I never could come to terms with the fact that my mother let that evil man destroy her, and she actually helped him do it.

I grieved over her death for years after she died, feeling there may have been something I could have done that would have made her life better. I never came up with any satisfactory answer that made me feel better. I loved her, and it was painful for me to watch her slowly die from the lifestyle she had chosen for herself knowing I was helpless to save her.

Ralph was a first class tyrant that apparently enjoyed torturing me because I wouldn't give in to what I thought was his stupid demands. It was like war between Ralph, mother, and me, a war that only ended when I got married at fifteen years old to get away from home, and began my own life of misery. It didn't end for my mother until she died.

She was like most abused women who never do anything until something drastic happens, she just accepted her station in life, and didn't try to make changes that would have made her life bearable, if not happy.

Ralph made my childhood a nightmare. The only good memories I have from that period of my life was the little time I got to spend with Mama Phillips, and Mr. Elliott as well as the short visits from dad who knew nothing about the nightmare life I was living, some of which was of my own making.

I defied Ralph at every turn. I resented him telling me what to do. The hate I felt for him was eating me alive. My mother could never protect me from his wrath. She thought I brought a lot of it on myself, through my hostility, and aggression, and she was right. I could never overcome my attitude toward him.

When I finally told dad about my childhood many years later it upset him, something I never meant to do. He said he was sorry he had left me in a situation that could have destroyed my life however; I never looked at my situation as being his fault, and I never blamed him for anything that happened to me when I was a child.

I told dad that it would be nice to be able to blame someone for all of the mistakes, I made in my life however; somewhere down the line we have to take responsibility for our own actions that cause negative things to happen to us, and I thought I had taken responsibility for my contribution to my abusive childhood in the only way I knew how.

I have never seen a situation where alcoholism in a family didn't cause chaos. I know that it had a lot to do with our family relationships however; there was nothing I could do about that.

What I could have done was to be more tolerant, and accepting of Ralph when I finally realized my mother would never leave him for good, instead of having the attitude that I would never accept anything he did whether it was good or bad.

There were times that I would try to accept him, but I was never successful in making it last. Even today, I am not very diplomatic about issues I disagree with.

I am thankful that through the entire trauma of my childhood, I survived it with the knowledge that I could withstand a lot more than I thought possible, and come out of it with minimal psychological damage.

MOONSHINER CABIN

I told dad the following story that made an impression on me that I have never forgotten. It was an experience where I came to realize that there were people who were worse off financially than we were, and most likely after generations are still living in the same way.

When I went back to the area thirty years later in the 1980s the houses didn't look any different, except they had a television antenna on the roof, and some had a new car sitting in the yard. I imagine they still haven't changed very much now after thirty more years.

The story was about one of the times Ralph was hauling moonshine from across Amicalola Falls near Ellijay Georgia, to bootleggers in Forsyth County when he took us with him, and it became an exciting adventure I will never forget.

We knew he was going to buy liquor, what we didn't know was that we would have to ford a creek, get the car stuck, and see how real mountain folk lived.

We didn't have a flashlight at first when we got out of the car, it was pitch black, we couldn't see each other, let alone where we were going, and we were standing in water ankle deep.

Ralph struck matches to find the flashlight in the trunk of the car making it easier to find the foot log we had to use to get across the creek then we walked for what seemed to me like hour's, but was probably only several minutes in the dark before we got to our destination.

Along the way, we heard all kinds of animal sounds. The first ones we heard when we were near the creek Ralph said were frog's. I doubted his explaination however; I didn't have a better answer for what we heard.

When we got further up the road away from the creek the sounds changed, and got louder. It sounded like something from the wild kingdom and probably sounded a lot closer than it really was nevertheless, I felt like something was going to "grab me" at any minute.

Getting out of the car in the North Georgia Mountains was a scary experience and walking on a road so dark we couldn't see each other, a place where I knew there were mountain lions, bobcats, and black bears, my imagination was going crazy.

I knew we didn't have anything to protect us from any of those things should we encounter one. There are no words to explain how frightening that was to me. When we finally arrived at the cabin, it was well past mid-night, and the people who lived there had already gone to bed.

The cabin they lived in was different from anything I had ever seen before, and have never seen since. It had an odor I can't explain, and they had used pages out of a sears catalog, and newspapers for wallpaper. It looked as if the paper was used to cover cracks in the walls.

Their water came down from a spring on the mountain in a trough that ran through the wall into the kitchen where they had very little furniture; they had a wood stove, and a long homemade wood table with benches, and a homemade cabinet that held their dishes.

They had no living room. In the first room, we went in there was a wood heater, ladder-back chairs, a table with a radio on it, some old pictures on the wall, and an iron bed where their baby was sleeping everyone in the house got up, and no one got any more sleep that night.

They didn't seem to be bothered that we were there in the middle of the night. I guess they were accustomed to people coming late at night since their business wasn't exactly legal.

They had two teenage boys who got up to see what was going on. They were wearing dirty faded overalls that looked as though they had worn them for weeks.

Later we saw them chewing, and spitting tobacco. The dad was an older version of the boys, who acted as if they had never seen young girls before; they were overly friendly toward us. Mother and Ralph teased us about them for weeks afterward.

I don't know if the boys went to school. From what I saw, and heard I doubt they had ever seen the inside of a classroom. We had to stay at that cabin until the next morning, when Ralph and the man went up the road to get a tractor to pull the car out of the mud.

We didn't get any sleep, we were hungry, irritable, and were more than ready to go home by the time they got the car out of the creek, and loaded. It had been an interesting adventure, I had seen things I had never seen before, and would never see again, it wasn't anything I wanted to repeat soon.

Dad would have had a fit if he had known Ralph was taking us to places like that, and hauling liquor with us in the car, although there wouldn't have been anything he could have done therefore, it would have just caused trouble if I told him about it.

I knew I wouldn't tell dad about our adventure any time soon, I had learned my lesson about telling him anything that would cause him to confront Ralph.

I always felt he was apprehensive when dad would take us away from the house. He was probably afraid I would tell him what he was doing, and he certainly didn't want dad to know he was hauling moonshine, and involving us.

Dad's Second
Marriage

In February 1948, dad quit his job at the Yellow Cab Company where he had worked about four years, and went to work for Paul Conner at the Veteran Cab Company. Shortly after he was hired, he met another driver by the name of Jack Ross.

His friendship with Jack started a new phase in his life, one that would change his whole world in ways unimaginable to him at the time. He would later make a promise to Jack before his premature death, that he would live to regret.

He said Jack Ross was one of the best friends he ever had, and what happened to him was a terrible loss to humanity. He said he had never met anyone like him before or since. When he was telling me about Jack, and their friendship I realized their meeting was fate, and just another step on the path to his destiny.

After they became good friends Jack invited him to his home to meet his wife Sybil, and his son Jimmy. He soon learned Jack was not well; he had a brain tumor that later would require him to have brain surgery.

In 1948, brain surgery was a very risky process, and Jack worried about what would happen to his wife and son if he were to die. His doctor told him he had two choices, either have the surgery, giving him some possibility of recovery, or do nothing, and surely die.

After discussing his situation with his wife and explaining to her, that if he had the surgery the doctors were telling him he needed the prognosis was not good. However, if he didn't have it, he had no chance whatever of survival.

After the diagnosis is when they made the decision for him to have the surgery as soon as possible. Dad said one of the reason's for the decision to do it soon was that Jack was suffering unimaginable pain that would never go away.

He talked to dad about his dilemma, and told him he thought he was going to die, and that he was worried about what would happen to his wife and son if he were not there for them. Dad said he told him he would take care of them, and for him not to worry about that, and try to get well.

Jack Ross had the brain surgery that resulted in his death. A few months after Jack died Dad and Sybil were married. He explained to me that this marriage was one of his weak moments that he lived to regret.

He made a promise to his friend that he would look after his family if he were to die, and he had tried to fulfill that promise the only way he knew how, although he soon realized it was a promise he shouldn't have made.

He said it didn't take long for him to realize the relationship with Sybil was not working; she had a different outlook on life than he did, and he knew he should have found a more reasonable solution than marriage to look out for Jack's family.

He said she was a good cook, and housekeeper, but he found out right away that she was not the kind of woman he needed in his life. She always had an excuse when he questioned her about where she went while he was at work. He didn't believe her answers when other cab driver's were always telling him about seeing her places she denied going to.

He liked her parents although he thought they covered up for her. They would keep Jimmy while he was at work, allowing her to do things behind his back. She would always be home when he got there, although she could not hide the fact that she had not been there the entire day, and she would never admit the truth when he confronted her with it.

Knowing how dad was about truthfulness I understand why after catching her in lie after lie, he knew he would never be able to trust her. He said he suspected she had other men in her life, she continually did things that made him distrust her, but he never actually caught her with anyone.

He said they were not compatible enough to have a successful marriage, and he should have recognized that fact before he made the promise to Jack Ross, however, it didn't become reality to him until after the deed was done, and he had married her.

THE SECRET

O ne hot day in August 1949, my mother and her husband
started acting very secretively about something refusing
to tell us what was happening, they were buying an
Atlanta newspaper every day.

This was a very unusual thing for them to do, and especially for
my mothers husband Ralph, I had never known him to be interested
in anything printed in a newspaper, and when we asked them what
was going on they refused to tell us. We never imagined it could have
anything to do with our dad.

My sister and I were curious, especially after so many unusual visits with family we didn't visit often had occurred three days in a row.
On the way to their house, they would stop to buy another newspaper

that they were careful to keep us from seeing, then when we got there, they didn't let us stay inside to listen to their conversation.

We knew something was wrong, but they were not telling us what it was. The fourth day we went to the home of another family member where the secret talks and newspaper reading continued without telling us why.

When they made us stay outside this time, we went to visit the children who lived next door, as soon as the mother realized we were there, she called me to come inside and talk to her. She started asking me questions about my dad that I found strange, because I was not aware she knew him.

Then she proceeded to tell me my dad was in jail for hitting a famous woman by the name of Margaret Mitchell who was the author of a book I had never heard of before, and she told me that if she dies they will probably electrocute him.

That was when I started screaming at her that I didn't think she was telling the truth, my mother had not told me anything like that. At that point, when I was screaming at the neighbor Betty ran to get mother and Ralph telling them to come next door, and that they had better hurry, because I was screaming at the neighbor, and she didn't know what was wrong with me.

When mother asked why I was so upset I told her what that woman had told me, and it made her furious. She didn't hesitate to tell the woman she didn't appreciate her taking it upon herself to tell me something that was none of her business, that if she had wanted me to know about it, she would have told me.

My mother no longer had any choice she had to tell me what the woman was talking about, she told me that dad was arrested for hitting a rich and famous woman with his car, and that he was out of jail on bond, she told me not to believe everything that woman had said. It was then that I began to settle down a little.

I didn't completely believe what I heard until dad told me much later that he was safe, and for me not to worry about him. Mother said the reason she hadn't told me was because she wanted to protect me from finding out about it until she knew all of the details.

She knew how much I loved my dad, and she knew I would not react to the news very well. She now realized she had made a mistake by not telling me, she knew she couldn't hide what was happening from me any longer.

She said she was sorry, and that she should have told me when it first happened, then she proceeded to tell me everything she had read in the newspapers. Until after his trial conviction, and imprisonment I didn't hear anything from him personally.

Everything other people were telling me in addition to what I overheard mother and Ralph talking about, and what we were reading in the newspapers really frightened me.

The man the newspapers were describing was not the dad I had always known. I had never seen the man they described as a "drunken taxicab driver, grim faced and un-smiling" a man they were calling "murderer".

What was being published in the newspapers about him really scared me. Without hearing it from him personally, I didn't know what they were doing to him, I was afraid there was more to the situation than my mother was telling me.

After Margaret Mitchell died the newspaper headlines were full of wild statements such as "Gravitt Charged with Murder" making it sound as if he had deliberately hit and killed her. I had never heard of "Gone with the Wind", and I had no idea how important Margaret Mitchell was to Atlanta Society. In the country where we lived, most people had no idea who she was, and had never heard about the book or the movie.

It soon became real to me when the media and the public started demanding the harshest possible punishment for him "electrocution". I didn't understand how they could kill my dad because he had an accident.

I had seen enough in my young life that I didn't have much respect for the law. I believed they would do whatever was in their best interest if they thought they could get away with it. I find it ironic how accurate I was about the ethic's of law enforcement when I was only ten years old.

That was one of the most traumatic periods of my life. It was a time that I thought I might lose my dad forever, and there was nothing I could do to help him.

This was the beginning of forty-five years of the local newspaper's, and the public torture of Hugh Dorsey Gravitt. Every year on the week of August 11 he would get unwanted phone calls from people harrassing him, and from newspapers wanting him to make a statement about the death of Margaret Mitchell.

My dad was treated like a rabid dog by the newspaper's especially the Atlanta Journal where Margaret Mitchell and John Marsh had been employed in the past, and were long time friends of the editor Angus Perkerson and his wife Medora.

In my research about her death and their relationship with the newspaper community I know there were some of them who knew Margaret and John and their habit of jaywalking, and drinking alcohol that they never publicly admitted.

I have never understood how so many people could know so much about the background of Margaret Mitchell and John Marsh and never had the curiosity to question the unusual circumstances of her death, and the facts in the case against my dad that were mostly manufactured lies.

I never saw one official interview of the man Margaret and John had a dinner engagement with on August 11,1949 that John cancelled with the excuse that Margaret wasn't feeling well enough to go out to dinner.

Not only was the fact that John and not Margaret cancelled their dinner engagement enough to draw attention to this happening on the evening when she received the fatal injury that led to her death, but he admitted going to the movie was his idea.

This to anyone who knew them, especially her brother should have known that Margaret Mitchell not John Marsh always made the decision when they went out to any public function. It should have raised a red flag that something was wrong with the scenario for the whole day.

DEATH SCENE

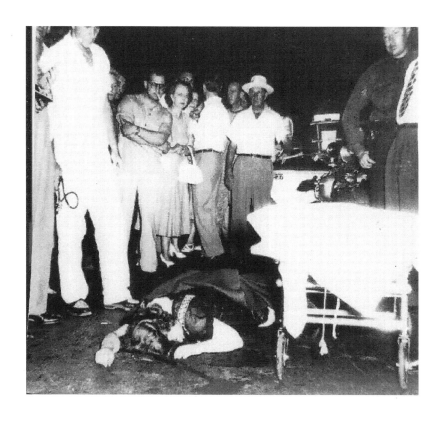

T he police photo of Margaret Mitchell lying on Peachtree Street in Atlanta Georgia on August 11, 1949, after being hit by a 1949 Ford driven by Hugh Dorsey Gravitt seen in the photo standing with his back turned talking to someone behind him.

John Marsh husband of the victim is standing behind the gurney talking to a policeman looking at the body of his wife. The medical tech standing holding a stethoscope looking down at the body of Margaret Mitchell showing that no one was rendering aid to the victim, or had even bothered to turn her over from where she fell when she was hit, inferring she was dead at the scene.

Dad told me he thought she was dead immediately after he hit her, and that it was covered up for five day's giving her family time to attend to her affairs. This police photo says more than any words I can ever say about when Margaret Mitchell actually died.

The lies and cover-up of when she died could be one reason Fulton County has kept her autopsy, and the record of dad's trial sealed for more than sixty-three years. Covering up conspiracy, and corruption to keep anyone from knowing she was killed instantly, and to convict Hugh Dorsey Gravitt for crimes he did not commit.

Dad said, that unforgettable day August 11, 1949, which turned out to be the worst day of his life was uneventful for the most part just normal routine after getting off work at 4: pm he had a beer with another driver, something he rarely did because of stomach ulcers that he had suffered from his entire adult life, that he had surgery to correct in his twenties after he almost died.

He would occasionally have a beer, and when he did, he suffered the consequences. He also had to be selective about what he ate, or chance ending up back in the hospital with his bleeding ulcers.

When he got home his wife Sybil told him, her four-year-old son Jimmy was sick with a fever. They called the doctor, and was given a prescription that dad was going to take to a pharmacy on Peachtree Street to get filled.

He told Sybil he didn't have enough money on him to pay for the medicine the doctor had prescribed for Jimmy, and that on his way to the pharmacy he would have to go to the taxicab company, to borrow some money from his boss to pay for it.

While she cooked their evening meal, he showered and got ready to go. After they ate, he left to go back to the cabstand. His boss had already left for the day, but four other drivers Jack Burns, James Trammel, Jack Bremer, and Cecil Vaughn were still there. He borrowed some money from Jack Burns, and left the cabstand a little after 8: pm.

Having been a cab driver in Atlanta for five years he was aware of pedestrians, and especially jaywalkers, and the unpredictable things they would do.

However, he never expected what happened next. He said he was traveling north on Peachtree Street, in heavy traffic, and had passed Thirteenth Street behind another car. When the car in front of him moved to the left crossing the center white line to go around pedestrian's in mid block that he could not see until that car moved over.

Dad said he was not speeding, he was just following the car in front of him, and he said neither of them was going more than the speed limit.

He said the car in front of him had slowed down, and crossed over the center white line to go around a man and woman standing in the middle of the street, he said when that car slowed down he had to slow down also.

He and the other car had slowed down below the speed limit before they approached the pedestrians, who were in the middle of the block on Peachtree Street, not at a crosswalk, or at the intersection, they were in the middle of the street standing dead still, the man with his back toward the curb facing the woman at a place where they were not supposed to be as shown in the drawing on the accident report.

Dad said when he saw the two pedestrian's Margaret Mitchell and John Marsh in front of him he had no idea he was seconds away from hell, a fate he could not even imagine

There was no valid legal reason for anyone to be in the middle of Peachtree Street jaywalking in heavy traffic unless they had an ulterior motive to cross the street at that particular time, under those particular circumstances. My dad said it was the perfect way to commit a murder, and get away with it.

Accident Report with Drawing Pg 1.

Accident Report pg 2.

Motor Vehicle Death Statistical Report

This work sheet shows Margaret Mitchell fatal injury dated Aug.12, 1949

Dad said as soon as the car in front of him moved over and he saw the pedestrian's in the street he blew his horn, and hit his brakes, slowing down well below the speed limit. He said he was straddling the white center line when one of the pedestrians a woman "appeared" to run backwards into the pathway of his car.

Dad said, after he hit her as he stood looking down at her lying motionless in the street, he had a terrible sinking feeling in the pit of his stomach while praying she was alive, and would survive he feared that wasn't possible. She wasn't moving or making a sound, he said he thought she was dead.

Her husband said he cradled, and comforted her while waiting for the ambulance to arrive, dad said that was a lie, that no one including John Marsh touched her before the ambulance arrived, and the medic who came with the ambulance took her pulse, and listened for a heartbeat without turning her over, before he stood up without rendering any kind of medical aid.

Afterward no one touched her again until finally after a considerable amount of time had passed they picked her up put her in the ambulance and took her to the hospital.

Dad said, he thought the ambulance would never get there, and when they did arrive, there was no medical aid given to her making him think she was already dead.

For several critical minutes her husband, the police officer, and the emergency people just stood around discussing who she was, and what had happened instead of administering medical aid then rushing her to the hospital as they would normally do in an emergency situation.

Dad said there was entirely too much time wasted doing nothing to help her while there was a chance she was still alive. When the medical person who came in the ambulance made no effort to provide her any medical assistance the only reasonable assumption for him was that she was dead on the scene, and there was no hurry to get her to the hospital.

He said they were making pictures of her when all they should have been interested in was getting her medical attention, he said her husband was not insisting they get her to the hospital, he was busy talking to the police, and pointing his finger at him.

Dad questioned why John Marsh didn't demand they take her to the hospital immediately. Was it because he knew she was dead immediately after the ambulance arrived?

In 1949, a brain injury of the magnitude she suffered was in the hand of God. The medical profession was not very skilled in handling serious brain injuries at that time.

Dad said because John Marsh "introduced the element of her importance' he blindsided the police, and the medical people who had come with the ambulance to her disadvantage by trying to draw the attention of the police away from himself and direct it to the driver of the car that hit her.

He said the police officer who arrested him knew the alcohol smelled at the scene was not coming from him. He said it was coming from the victim and her husband. And while all of that was taking place dad said he was in panic mode, because no one was trying to help the injured woman who was face down in the street.

Her husband told the police his name was John Marsh and that the woman was his wife Margaret Mitchell Marsh who was the author of "Gone with the Wind" all the while pointing dad out as the driver of the car that hit her.

What John Marsh was telling the policeman didn't make much sense to him at the time, because he didn't know anything about "Gone with the Wind", and definitely didn't know who Margaret Mitchell was, therefore, he couldn't have known the significance of the details John Marsh was giving to the police officer at that time.

Several minutes after the incident occurred other police officer's arrived, one of them with a camera, that police officer was more interested in making pictures of her lying in the street, and getting the names of the people who were standing in a circle around her asking if they saw what happened, to be concerned about her survival.

Dad said he had never seen a live injured victim of an accident left lying in the street while the police questioned bystanders as they had done in this case. He said their actions were inexcusable, and probably in violation of the law if she was alive.

He said the incident happened at approximately 8:20 pm and it took until almost 9: pm to get her to the hospital that was only minutes away. He said he was so upset over the whole procedure he felt as though he couldn't breathe.

He said that by the time they finally took her to the hospital his fear was that if she had not died instantly when he hit her "she had died" while they stood around discussing who she was.

He had not seen her move, and he couldn't imagine any other reason, other than that she was dead to explain the delay in taking her to the hospital, and the medic that came with the ambulance failing to render medical aid looked very suspicious to him.

As soon as they realized who she was the medical emergency mode, and police procedure went out the window, and the celebrity mode took over putting her critical injuries on hold.

The intelligent man John Marsh was, he knew if he made the police aware of her identity right away it would slow everything down making her chance of recovery less likely.

Pointing his finger at dad as the guilty party took the focus away from him, making sure the police didn't take a closer look at himself as a possible suspect.

From the beginning of my research I learned John Marsh suffered from a Psychosomatic illness and I suspected he had psychopathic traits as well, and that was when my research led me to my first interest in Psychiastrist Hervey Cleckly in "Mask Of Sanity" and other sources in that field, and everything I learned about John over the years confirmed my personal thoughts about the extent his mental illness.

His actions while his wife lay injured in the street were those of a person who could not identify with, or understand the feelings of others, his actions were how someone who felt no empathy for her would have acted in that kind of situation.

He showed no apparent compassion or sympathy for the suffering of his wife. When dad told me how John acted after his wife was critically injured, and was possibly dead I remembered about John having a weird psychosomatic illness and I looked up mental illness and learned that was how a psychopath would have acted.

Dad said he had never seen anyone whose loved one was possibly dying as calm and unemotional as her husband was. His actions were certainly not what he would consider "normal" under those circumstances.

The police didn't even talk to dad until after the ambulance left the scene with her. They had done most of their talking to John Marsh who left with the ambulance to take his wife to the hospital. Then they took dad to the police station where he was threatened, fingerprinted, and booked.

He said the same photographer from the scene was also at the jail with a camera, and they set him up for what happened next. He said one of the police officer's was talking to him in a friendly manner as they were leaving the room where he had been fingerprinted.

They stopped when they got into a hallway as they continued their conversation he leaned against a cell door. At that time, the police photographer appeared again, and told him to smile, and without thinking, he smiled, and his picture was made.

Celestine Sibley a Columnist from the Atlanta Constitution who was the only person from the many newspapers that were screaming for my dads' blood who thought the incident that killed Margaret Mitchell was not his fault.

She said that picture made in the jail when they took dad to be fingerprinted went out over the wires and "shocked the world".

She said people believed he was a heartless killer, and he was the opposite, he was grief stricken, and told her many times over the years that he didn't even know he was smiling; he was so stunned over what had happened.

Dad talked to her occasionally over the years after 1949. He said she was the only newspaper person he could talk with who didn't condemn him.

When the photo session was over two police officers took him into a room where they tried to scare him into telling them he was drunk by telling him it made no difference if he admitted it or not that if that woman dies we will charge you with "murder", and we will "electrocute "you.

He told them the truth; he had a beer before he left work at 4: pm more than four hours before the incident, then showered, and ate dinner after that. He never varied from that statement.

They told him the woman you hit is the most important author in Georgia, and probably the whole world, her name is Margaret Mitchell, she is rich and famous with social and political ties to this community. They told him he was in more trouble than he could even imagine, and as it turned out he could never in a million years have realized just how much trouble he was in until Chief Herbert Jenkins charged him with murder.

He said he just couldn't absorb everything they were telling him. They were trying to make it look like he had deliberately picked her out, and ran her down, when he actually had no idea who she was except what he had heard John Marsh telling the policeman at the scene who they were, and what he heard Marsh saying didn't mean much to him because he didn't know who they were anyway.

Dad told the police officers who questioned him that he had never heard of Margaret Mitchell or "Gone with the Wind" and didn't know anything about either one. Dad had very little education, and could not read well enough to read books, therefore he had never read Gone With The Wind, nor had he seen the movie.

He was a cab driver that worked seven days a week and he didn't socialize with his fares about movies or what was going on in Atlanta at the time. He just wasn't interested in that sort of thing. The only thing he had on his mind was where they were going and how much the meter was ringing up.

If any of the people who rode in his cab had talked about Margaret Mitchell and the movie it wouldn't have made any more sense to dad than it did when John Marsh was telling the police who they were at the scene of the incident. After he was arrested and the police told him who she was, and told him that if she died they would electrocute him he knew right away he was in a lot of trouble.

Even after he made bond and went home he still couldn't imagine the nightmare he would endure for the next forty-five years caused mostly by an unrelenting media for whatever their purpose they never let him forget.

Dad told me he repeatedly tried to make the police aware that his stepson was ill, and he was on his way to the pharmacy to get medicine for him. He asked them if someone could get the medicine, and take it to his wife. They just ignored his pleas, about his sick child; they were more interested in the fame of Margaret Mitchell.

They never did get the medicine for Jimmy he didn't get it until his mother came to the police station to get the prescription they had taken from dad, so there was no doubt about his destination, she took it to be filled herself.

He said the fear, and turmoil going through his mind while they were questioning him was like a nightmare while he was wide-awake. He said the full impact of what was about to happen to him had not hit him yet. The fury of the media, and public opinion was to come later.

This was just a preview of what he could expect until the trial was over and he went to prison. He said he was already upset, and after the encounter with the police, he was in worse shape, especially when they put him in protective custody because of threats on his life.

He couldn't sleep, he walked the floor of his cell, and prayed for the woman he hit to recover, although it was hard for him to think of her as alive after what he had seen at the scene.

The police told him she was alive, and he hoped they were telling him the truth. His fear was that if she really was dead they would electrocute him as they had threatened. He said all kind of nightmarish thoughts were running crazy through his mind, and he was terrified that he couldn't survive it.

He was worried about his sick child at home that needed the medicine he was on his way to get, and he prayed that everything would soon get back to normal however, his life never returned to normal.

The original charges imposed by traffic Judge Luke Arnold were drunk driving, speeding, violating state motor vehicle law, failure to yield the right of way to a pedestrian, driving on the wrong side of the street.

Judge Arnold acted with full knowledge that he was going against his own ruling that jaywalkers were liable in such situations. Garner Bonding Company posted his bond of $5,450 then they released him pending any changes in Margaret Mitchell's condition.

The police, and Prosecutor coverd-up the fact that she was drunk, and illegally jaywalking when she was hit, and that her husband was also jaywalking when he led her out into busy Peachtree Street at a time when she was not capable of making decisions for herself. Dad's attorney was virtually ineffective in his representation.

MARGARET MITCHELL
REPORTED DEAD

⟨decorative flourish⟩

O n August 16, 1949 shortly after noon the Atlanta Police notified dad that Margaret Mitchell had died at 11:59 am at Grady Memorial Hospital. His worst nightmare was set in motion, and it would last for forty-five years.

After he notified his Attorney A.L. Henson, and Garner Bonding Company he turned himself in to the Atlanta Police Department. He said what the newspapers were saying about him was being exaggerated, and was not what had actually happened to Margaret Mitchell.

When he went to turn himself in his thoughts were that either they were going to electrocute him, or at the very least they would lock him up and throw away the key was what he expected, I think that is what they would have done if they had thought they could get away with it.

He thought if he went to prison his life, as he had known it would be over, the fear he felt about what was going to happen to him was indescribable, and nothing was ever the same for him again. His life was in a shambles and he was too upset to figure out what was happening.

He knew there were unstable people out there who were threatening his life, that caused the jail to put him in protective custody prior to him making bond before Margaret Mitchell died, and now that she was dead he didn't know what to expect next.

He definitely didn't trust the Atlanta Police Department to protect him from the crazy people who wanted to kill him. Most of the police were not educated enough to investigate a high profile case such as this.

The following appeared on the front page of the Atlanta Constitution on August 17,1949. "Grim faced and silent Hugh D. Gravitt, 29 year old taxi-cab driver voluntarily surrendered to Atlanta Police headquarters yesterday two hours after the death of Margaret Mitchell where he was held without bond on a charge of murder".

Dad said when they charged him with murder he felt more fear than he had ever felt before in his life. The police officer who arrested him had told him if that woman you hit dies; we will electrocute you, and from the newspaper lies and the public outcry he believed it might happen.

He was afraid the way the local newspaper that both Margaret and John had worked for was making up stories to fit what they wanted it to be turning it into a circus like atmosphere that everyone believed for the truth.

The media was causing outrage from the public all over the world. The newspapers were full of unbelievable stories that were not true. The President of the United States, and the Governor of Georgia were demanding the harshest possible punishment for him.

He was afraid their involvement could actually allow the State of Georgia to follow through with the execution the Atlanta Police told him would happen to him if she died. It was total chaos for him, and he feared for his life.

At that point, he definitely didn't trust anyone. He knew he "wasn't drunk" when he hit her, and he "had not" been driving as fast as the police, and the newspapers said he was. All of the charges against him were fabricated lies that didn't closely resemble the truth. He had already figured out that he couldn't trust anyone in law enforcement, or anyone else.

He didn't know what horror would come next; he just knew that it would not be pleasant. Georgia's most famous, author Margaret Mitchell was dead, and people all over the world were condemning him for killing her.

He couldn't forget what the policemen who arrested him told him they would do to him if she died, he couldn't comprehend how they could execute him for a crime that his only participation in was to drive down Peachtree Street on his way to a pharmacy at the exact moment John Marsh was ready to throw his intoxicated wife under a moving car.

He said sleep was impossible that all he could do was walk the floor of his cell, and pray that there would be someone that he didn't know about, with enough credibility to question the circumstances of the charges against him. That person never materialized.

His prayers fell on deaf ears, and no one to this day has ever questioned her husbands involvement in her death until now. Everything I have researched about her death confirms what my dad told me.

He realized that it made no difference what he said or did it was too late to do anything about it that he was tried and convicted by corruption, and a conspiracy to cover-up what actually happened to her.

He was going to prison and his lawyers told him for his personal safety he could never talk about the facts in his case, he was warned until he was convinced to keep his mouth shut about what he knew about Margaret Mitchell's death, or he would suffer the consequences.

EVIDENCE DESTROYED

Why the police, and Margaret's brother Stephens Mitchell didn't question why John with the help of the janitor at their apartment complex, and their secretary Margaret Baugh "who was horrified" at what he was doing began destroying her belongings immediately after her funeral is mind boggling.

What was the hurry to do away with everything she owned immediately after her funeral instead of quietly mourning as would be expected of her husband, especially since he was so eager for everyone to think he was an invalid.

Why was burning her important papers and her clothes before anyone could get a look at them. Was he burning evidence? And why did he ask everyone she had written letters to destroy them along with all other correspondence from her?

John's actions immediately after Margaret's funeral was absolutely bizarre, and his motive for burning her belongings should have been thoroughly examined by her brother, and the police. What he was doing should have raised a red flag that alerted everyone that something wasn't right.

Why they didn't demand to know if destroying everything was her idea, and why she didn't she tell anyone other than John that she wanted everything destroyed after her death is questionable. If that was what she wanted why didn't she put it in her will that was written in her own hand in November 1948. Everything I've read tells me her brother did know, and most likely confronted John Marsh about it.

Was John so afraid the truth would come out that their relationship was nothing more than a "bargain" to write a book? And that his work on it was much more than "editing", and their unusual interactions with each other could be covered up by destroying everything to prevent anyone from learning how bizarre their relationship really was?

Dad's thoughts were that it was to "destroy evidence", and to remove her from his life forever, and that he may have been threatening her that he would tell the world the truth about the book and her personal life that she never wanted made public to continue his manipulation of her, and to control the money.

I cannot imagine a normal man with all of his literary experience, and education who couldn't understand the value to future generations the importance of preserving everything that had belonged to her.

Especially anything to do with "Gone with the Wind". According to one of her biographers Marianne Walker he told his mother years before that he was a very selfish person, and his actions after her death prove how selfish and deceptive he actually was. I don't believe John Marsh was a normal man. He had all of the trait's of a psychopath when he showed no empathy for his wife or anyone else.

War on Taxicab Drivers

When dad hit Margaret Mitchell he was not driving a cab as was reported by many newspapers, he was driving his personal car a 1949 Ford. Although the media spread the lie that a taxicab had hit Mitchell, and those lie's are still on the internet today.

The newspapers and the police tried to crucify him because he made his living driving a cab, and the politician's went after all cab drivers, and cab companies in Atlanta because of this incident.

Numerous cab driver's lost their job, and the Veteran Cab Company dad worked for and all other cab companies in Atlanta had their records pulled causing them as much trouble as possible Dad said I owe a lot to Paul Conner who was the president of the Veteran Cab Company he stood by me when they took my permit to drive a cab for life, and gave me a job fueling and working on cars, and that job was waiting for me when I got out of prison.

He said. if Paul Conner and his co-workers hadn't stood by him, he didn't know if he could have withstood the horrible nightmare his life had become. Knowing he had a job waiting for him when he got out of prison meant more to him than he could express in words.

When he got out of prison knowing he couldn't drive a cab, he had to compensate for the difference in the money he would be making. He did that by buying two car's that he leased to the cab company that extra money helped him make enough money to support his family.

On August 17,1949, Paul W. Conner made the statement to the Atlanta Constitution Newspaper that Hugh Gravitt was a good driver, and at least two-thirds of all cab operators probably had as many traffic violations against them as he had.

He had only four offenses in the eighteen months he had been driving for the Veteran Cab Company. Conner said any man driving 12 hours a day 365 days a year with only four violations on his record has done well.

In the Atlanta Newspaper on Sunday August 24,1949, dad's lawyer A.L.Henson said that minor Atlanta Official's and especially the police were attempting to persecute Hugh Gravitt in order to do what they thought the public wanted—to victimize him.

Henson said, "these people are taking advantage of the most regrettable incident of this decade to raise themselves in public esteem," I think he helped their cause by refusing to use the only defense dad had. I wonder what Prosecutor Paul Webb could have done that persuaded him to throw my dad to the "wolves."

Dad's lawyer A.L.Henson knew Margaret Mitchell was drunk when she drove her car to the theater, and was drunk when my dad hit and fatally injured her.

He knew Margaret Mitchell and John Marsh were jaywalking in violation of the traffic laws of Atlanta, yet he told dad it would hurt his case more than it would help it to make those violation's public. I find that unacceptable from the lawyer he paid to represent him.

Commenting on his twenty-four traffic violation's in the five years he had been driving a cab, Henson said all but two of the charges were of a petty nature and would not have come to the attention of the public if Margaret Mitchell had not been a celebrity.

He said that in "six or seven" of the charges he had been found "not guilty." As for the reckless driving charges he paid a small fine, and was acquitted on the other. Henson pointed out that before the recent tragedy dad had never been in an accident involving injury to another person.

His lawyer described dad as a good family man with no moral taint on his record. Dad told the court when he testified in his trial that the newspaper's and politician's had made a scapegoat out of him.

His lawyer's told the court that newspaper's magazine's and politician's were crucifying him, and were trying to walk to glory on the bones of those men driving cab's more than sixty cab driver's lost their job and livelihood because of their action's.

Dad testified that he was a former cab driver, but was now a service man in the company shop of the cab company for which he formerly drove. He clearly stated in an emphatic way that after the newspaper's all over the country have indicted me, I can't get anything but a laborer's job.

He told the court that witnesses, even the doctor who had written the prescription for his stepson on the night of the incident were afraid to come down and testify for him because of the newspapers, and publicity

His lawyer A.L.Henson told the jury that dad had been pummeled and beaten by falsehood's and innuendos and punished far more already than you could possibly punish him by giving him the full penalty.

Henson stated, "this poor devil has been quartered and drawn already, since the incident on August 11, his life has been a hideous nightmare. His words didn't come close to describing the real horror and nightmare dad had suffered at the hands of the police, the state, and the public.

His other Lawyer Gower singled out Margaret Shannon of the Atlanta Journal as being unnecessarily brutal in her attack on Gravitt. The Journal continually attacked him until the trial was over and he was in prison.

Knowing all of this discrimination against him why didn't his lawyer's follow up with motions, and legal documents to get the case thrown out? That's simple dad, said it was because not only was his life being threatened, so were his lawyer's.

I think they were as helpless as dad was to stop the State of Georgia, and Prosecutor Paul Webb who were determined to convict him regardless of the fact that Margaret Mitchell was drunk, and incapable of making decisions on her own, her husband John Marsh was at fault for the incident that took her life, even if he hadn't shoved her backwards into dad's car.

When John Marsh let his drunk wife drive them from their apartment to the place they parked on Peachtree Street, then proceeded to lead her out into the street jaywalking without regard to her safety he became legally responsible.

FRAUDULENT
INDICTMENT

When Investigating Officer Sgt. Jack Eaves and M.C. Faulkner questioned dad he admitted he had one beer before he home for the day. He said he drank the beer at least four hours before the incident when he hit Margaret Mitchell.

In the newspapers and the prosecutor's indictment that beer turned into liquor, and they had charged him with being drunk. They took his honesty about having a beer earlier in the day and used it against him.

The doctor, who testified for the prosecution said, that he would not have felt the effects of the beer he had consumed more than four hours earlier.

The headline in the Atlanta Constitution on Wednesday November 16, 1949, written by Marjory Smith "Gravitt Speed Set at 50 by Marsh as Trial Opens." She described John Marsh as a snowy-haired, mild mannered man who told the Fulton Superior Court Jury in Atlanta Georgia "he was afraid he would see for the rest of his life the automobile which struck down his wife Margare Mitchell Marsh on Peachtree Street".

John Marsh was the principle witness who testified before the Grand Jury, and testified against dad at trial. He testified under oath that he was traveling at a high rate of speed, adding that if he was going less than fifty miles per hour he was very much mistaken. {The accident report contradicts his sworn statement. And he didn't admit his culpability in leading his intoxicated wife out into Peachtree Street jaywalking.}

No one asked him why he and his wife were crossing busy Peachtree Street in the middle of the block, instead of at the corner, which would have put them closer to the theatre where they were suposedly going to see a movie.

If dad's Lawyer A.L. Henson had tried to ask him questions that would have put him or his wife in a bad light, the judge would have stopped him. The court catered to John Marsh, they even provided him with a place to lie down if he became too tired to continue. This shows just how far he went to mislead the court about his physical condition.

With everything I know about this case it seems ludicrous to me that not one person questioned Marsh about his participation in his wife's death. Not even her brother Stephens Mitchell never suspected anything, if he did he never said anything publicly about it that I could find.

John Marsh was much too inteligent to believe a car going 50 miles per hour could hit his wife , or anyone and not cause a scratch or any damage to the car, and if she had been standing upright as he said she was, there would have definately been some kind of damage to the car. He lied to the court to make sure they convicted my dad for crimes for which he was not guilty.

Dad told me John Marsh not only lied to the court about how his wife was killed, he deliberately destroyed evidence when he burned her clothes on the day after her funeral. He said, a man that would go to those extremes given the opportunity would commit other crimes.

John Marsh and Margaret Mitchell were not above blatantly lying. They conspired to lie to Angus Perkerson who was the editor of the Atlanta Journal Newspaper to get him to hire Margaret as a reporter.

They lied to the editor of the newspaper about her experience and her typing abilities to get her a job. If he would lie about that he wouldn't have a problem lying about the circumstances of the incident that killed her.

Both of them lied easily when it was for something that would benefit them financially. Just as they lied to get her hired at the Atlanta Journal. Anyone who has read the biographies of her life, with emphasis on who they were, and how they reacted to every known issue their entire life, it isn't hard to figure out what kind of people they were.

Before the Grand Jury indicted dad on August 23, 1949, the charge was reduced to involuntary manslaughter, and his bond was reduced to five thousand dollars. Prosecutor Paul Webb said that at no time during the grand jury session did they contemplate a murder indictment."That was a lie" otherwise the Police Chief Herbert Jenkins wouldn't have filed a charge of murder against him in the first place?

The evidence presented to the grand jury to indict Hugh Dorsey Gravitt on a state charge of drunk driving, failure to yield the right of way to pedestrian "Margaret Mitchell Marsh" driving on the wrong side of the street, and speeding was fraudulent as stated on the indictment.

The accident report and the indictment are proof that if the grand jury had seen the actual official accident report my dad signed on August 11, 1949 they couldn't have indicted him. After he was indicted and bound over to the court for prosecution the actual accident report was then filed with the Fulton County Clerk of Court on August 24, 1949; the day after he was indicted.

I haven't been able to find anything that says Prosecutor Paul Webb ever looked at John Marsh as a possible suspect although everyone involved in the case knew he should have been charged with jaywalking, and endangering the life of his intoxicated wife by leading her out into traffic on Peachtree Street. My question is why didn't they give him a sobriety test, and charge him with jaywalking at the very least?

John Marsh playing an invalid in the presence of the police, and the newspapers knew what had actually happened to his wife, and judging by his actions he must have thought others could also know.

When he received the grand jury summons his reaction reflected guilt, he couldn't be sure what he would be questioned about. He didn't know what dad had seen, and had possibly reported to the authorities.

He hired Attorney Henry Troutman to accompany him to the Grand Jury hearing to defend him if he should be questioned about his involvement in his wife's death.

The other witnesses testifying in this case didn't have an attorney present. They knew they hadn't committed any crime therefore they didn't need to be represented by legal counsel. Not true of John Marsh he did feel he needed an attorney present.

The witnesses having been prepared for their testimony by the prosecutor knew they were to only answer the questions they were asked therefore; the grand jury was never made aware that Margaret

Mitchell and John Marsh were "jaywalking" or that they were not crossing at the end of the block as stated in the indictment.

I find it strange that John didn't ask his brother-in-law Attorney Stephens Mitchell to accompany him to the grand jury hearing. He had always been the one John and Margaret turned to when they needed any kind of legal assistance. However; this particular time when he knew what he had done, and thought there was a possibility the grand jury might also know that he had killed his wife, for obvious reasons he couldn't use the services of his brother in-law

John Marsh knew what his legal culpability was in the death of his wife; he knew he was the one who led her out into busy Peachtree Street jaywalking in the middle of the block when she was drunk, and incapable of making decisions on her own.

He made the police and everyone else believe his wife drove the car the ten blocks from their apartment then parked at a location on busy Peachtree Street where they would have to cross multiple lanes of traffic to get to the theatre where they were supposedly going.

That is not something a sensible sober person would do unless going to the theatre was not the purpose for being there in the first place. Dad said John Marsh knew perfectly well why they were there.

When they got out of the car, and started to cross Peachtree Street John said he looked both ways to see if anything was coming, he said they saw "two cars" already abreast of Thirteenth Street coming their way.

You have to ask yourself why he would continue across the street after he saw cars coming, unless he intended to throw his intoxicated wife in front of one of them.

Judging how long it would take the cars to reach them he proceeded to "lead her to her death" by crossing Peachtree Street in the middle of the block where there was no street light or crosswalk.

When he got to the middle of the street he stopped and faced Margaret waiting for the first car to go by that was when dad said he shoved her backwards, and her head hit the bumper of his car causing the brain damage that killed her. There was absolutely no way he could have avoided hitting her.

Why the Prosecutor Paul Webb, Police Chief Herbert Jenkins and Judge Luke Arnold didn't find the actions of John Marsh suspicious shows complete incompetence, and failure to carry out their duties to enforce the law.

Dad told me everything he could remember about the day he hit Margaret Mitchell and everything that happened to him as a result of it. He said anything he couldn't remember to tell me I could get from the newspapers, and from the Fulton County Courthouse. After his death I discovered the trial records were sealed by the court, and I couldn't get access to them. They are still sealed today.

After looking at the false charges on the indictment and the way Judge Arnold ruled in dad's case he never stood a chance against that kind of corruption. If there had been any kind of competent investigation into the incident when Margaret Mitchell was fatally injured the truth would have surfaced.

There was no real investigation, they had my dad, and they threw everything they thought would stick at him, regardless of whether it was based on fact, or if it was fabricated lies by the prosecutor.

His defense counsel apparently cooperated with the prosecution, and refused to bring up the relevant facts in the case that would have exonerated him from prosecution, on the basis that she was drunk, and jaywalking.

They needed a scapegoat, and who better than a lowly taxicab driver with no social or political standing would make a better one. If not for the fame, and social standing of Margaret Mitchell in Atlanta, and the world, my dad would never have been indicted for her death.

I don't believe there was anyone in the legal system in Atlanta Georgia in 1949 that had the competence or the integrity to do the right thing in the case against him. If they had been competent enough to know there was a problem with the case, their actions would have been the same because of her fame and standing in the community.

The president of the United States, the governor of Georgia, politicians, the media, and the public, were screaming for dad to get the harshest punishment possible, even asking for execution.

The indictment itself is representative of the prosecutor's office lacking the skill, and competence to draft the indictment against him even though they were using fabricated, and fraudulent charges to insure his conviction.

The Motor-Vehicle-Accident-Death-Statistica-Transcript shows Margaret Mitchell had been drinking. John Marsh said she also drove her car ten blocks from her apartment, if that is true she drove drunk, and was drunk when dad struck, and fatally injured her.

Following is the Traffic Code for the City of Atlanta in 1949. When it is compared to the accident report, it plainly shows that the failure to yield the right of way did not apply in my dad's case, because Margaret Mitchell and John Marsh were jaywalking in violation of the law when she was hit and fatally injured.

Code of the City of Atlanta Section 86-501 {a} Pedestrians Right of Way. The driver of any vehicle shall yield the right of way to a pedestrian crossing any roadway within any marked crosswalk. Or within any unmarked crosswalk at the end of a block, except at inter-sections where the movement of traffic is being regulated by a police officer or traffic signal, or at any point where a pedestrian tunnel or overhead crossing has been provided.

Margaret Mitchell and John Marsh crossed Peachtree Street in the middle of the block as shown in the police drawing on the acci-dent report, they were not crossing at an intersection, or within any unmarked crosswalk at the end of a block, nor was the traffic being regulated by a police officer or a traffic signal, there was no pedes-trian tunnel or overhead crossing, they were blatantly "jaywalking" in violation of the lawful traffic ordinance of the City of Atlanta.

Prosecutor Paul Webb was aware of these facts; however, he continued to lie on the indictment to make sure that my dad was punished for crimes he didn't commit proven by the following traffic code in 1949.

Code of the City Of Atlanta Section 88-708 {a} unless impractical because of obstructions, or when passing another vehicle, operators shall drive upon the right half of the roadway at all times. This provision shall not apply upon one way streets.

Margaret Mitchell and John Marsh were the "obstacles" that caused dad to move across the center white line to go around them. One of the charges against him was driving on the wrong side of the road, a false charge that prosecutor Paul Webb knew was false.

Jaywalking in Atlanta in 1949 was illegal unless you were famous with the right connections. Pedestrians crossing streets any place other than an officially designated crosswalk assume liability for accidents under a ruling handed down by Traffic Judge Luke Arnold.

The following Jaywalking cases in Atlanta, some of them took place on August 17.1949 the day after Margaret Mitchell died shows that my dad's case was not looked at on the same level as the following cases. For the rule of law to work it has to be applied to everyone equally.

John Marsh is the person who should have been arrested for leading his intoxicated wife out into the middle of the block on busy Peachtree Street jaywalking, and shoving her in front of my dad's moving car. Dad said that explains why he hired a lawyer to accompany him when he was summoned to appear before the grand jury.

Hugh Dorsey Gravitt had the right to equal protection under the law and it was not upheld in the case against him. Judge Luke Arnold didn't apply his own ruling on jaywalking. In my dad's case, and the traffic charges filed against him should never have been filed.

The following cases, some of them tried before Judge Arnold, I found very interesting. Especially the ones he ruled on within a few days of ruling in the case of State Of Georgia v. Hugh Dorsey Gravitt when those circumstances had to be fresh in his mind.

The Atlanta Constitution reported the following jaywalking accident's on August 17, 1949, the day after Margaret Mitchell died, that shows how Judge Arnold ruled differently in those incident's than he did in dads' case. Although most of them did not involve a death, the traffic laws were the same.

Judge Arnold dismissed charges of reckless driving-accident and leaving the scene of an accident against J.M. Turner a twenty-four year old sailor who lived at 224 Duke Road. Turner hit two pedestrians nineteen year old Barbara West and Angel Chaufon who were crossing Peachtree Street about one hundred feet from the intersection of Fifth Street inflicting leg injuries on both victims.

After the accident Turner left the scene and drove about three hundred feet down the street, parked his car and returned to the scene on foot. The arresting officer said the vehicle a 1940 Ford Convertible Coupe was damaged on the left side. My dad's car didn't have a scratch on it after he hit Margaret Mitchell. This should have been something important that the police should have considered when determining how fast he was going when he hit her.

Judge Arnold fined both victim's Barbara West and Angel Chaufon twelve dollars each on charges of jaywalking, then he suspended the charges. Arnold said both of them were crossing the street "illegally" when the car struck them. Those same laws apparently didn't apply to Margaret Mitchell and John Marsh six days earlier.

The two Atlanta Police Officer's Sgt. Jack Eaves, and Patrolman M.C. Faulkner who were the investigators in this accident are the same two who arrested dad, and they along with Judge Arnold played a huge part in the indictment and the malicious prosecution of Hugh Dorsey Gravitt that followed.

The second jaywalking case on August 17, 1949 the day after Margaret Mitchell died was a seventy-six year old negro man Goldie Sims, who received a fractured collarbone and numerous cuts and bruises when he was struck by a truck driven by thirty-seven year old Roy T. Jones, of Gordon Road S.W. Goldie Sims was booked for jaywalking. The driver of the truck was "not charged". Goldie Sims wasn't rich and famous with political and social influence in Atlanta Georgia; therefore, the law was applied correctly in his case.

The traffic laws on jaywalking in Atlanta, and surrounding area's are the same today that they were in 1949. On November 17, 2008, a mother crossing South Cobb Drive outside a crosswalk with four children in tow, when a driver struck and killed her four-year-old daughter, the driver was not charged. The police charged the mother

Altamesa Walker of Marietta with involuntary manslaughter, and reckless conduct.

On Tuesday September 21, 2010, at about 7: am while crossing Lenox Road near Piedmont, a white Honda struck forty-four year old pedestrian Sybil Nurse, who was transported by ambulance to Grady Hospital where she was reportedly in stable condition with a broken leg and other injuries. Police spokesperson Kim Jones said the "driver was not charged" however they did charge Sybil Nurse with "jaywalking".

An eighty-two year old woman Ruby Young and another pedestrian were crossing the street in the middle of the block on 10th Street in Atlanta Georgia on November 28, 2010 when she was fatally injured, and died the next day. Because she was "jaywalking" the driver of the car was "not charged".

A Cobb County Georgia mother Raquel Nelson was convicted of homicide second degree, and reckless conduct for crossing a roadway "jaywalking" where there was no marked crosswalk with her three children when her son A. J. Nelson was killed, the mother and her younger daughter suffered minor injuries, the older daughter was not hurt. They were trying to cross a four-lane Austell Georgia Road to get to their apartment after getting off a Cobb County transit bus.

Jerry L. Guy the driver of the car left the scene and later someone turned him in. He admitted hitting the four year old boy plead guilty to hit-and-run and served six months in jail, and the remainder of his five year sentence on probation. That man didn't serve as much time as.Hugh Gravitt did when he hit Margaret Mitchell.

The jaywalking cases I have referenced above where the driver of the vehicle was not charged are only a sampling of the numerous others that have occurred in Atlanta from 1949, until 2011. Proving the same laws that protected other drivers involved in jaywalking incidents did not apply to Hugh Gravitt.

STATE OF GEORGIA, COUNTY OF FULTON.

IN THE SUPERIOR COURT OF SAID COUNTY.

THE GRAND JURORS selected, chosen and sworn for the County of Fulton, to-wit:

1 _____, Foreman

1 C. L. EMERSON, Foreman

2 WILBUR F. GLENN, Asst. Foreman   13 CLIFFORD L. NEWTON
3 HOLCOMBE T. GREEN, Secretary   14 J. F. CLOUD, SR.
4 D. J. KANE, Asst. Secretary   15 HENRY G. GLOER
5 C. H. McGAUGHEY   16 WILLIAM C. BURNETT
6 L. T. SPRADLING   17 E. D. JESTER
7 ROBERT J. LOFTIN   18 J. V. SUMMERS
                                         19 W. H. SPIVEY
9 C. M. STOVALL   20 W. D. TAULMAN
10 H. W. BOOZER   21 ARTHUR W. DUKE
11 WILLIAM B. DUNN   22 JAMES T. WHITNER
12 W. M. EMMERT   23 R. B. WILBY

11 _____

12 _____ 23 _____

in the name and behalf of the citizens of Georgia, charge and accuse

HUGH D. GRAVITT

with the offense of:—

INVOLUNTARY MANSLAUGHTER (Felony)

for that said accused, in the County of Fulton and State of Georgia, on the

11th _____ day of _____ August _____, 19 40

with force and arms, did unlawfully, and without any intention to do so, kill Mrs.
____sh, while accused was engaged in the commission of an unlawful act,
which might probably produce such a consequence, in an unlawful manner; in tha

Accused did drive and operate an automobile along and upon Peachtree Stree
at the intersection of Thirteenth Street, Northeast, both being public streets
and highways in the City of Atlanta, Georgia, said intersection being within t
City Limits of the City of Atlanta, Georgia, said county, and did violate the
law in the following respects:

(a) Accused did drive and operate said automobile along and upon said
Peachtree Street at a greater rate of speed than twenty-five (25) miles per
hour, in violation of the lawful ordinance of the City of Atlanta, which provided as follows, -

" Code of the City of Atlanta. Section 88-703. RESTRICTIONS AS TO
SPEED. Any person driving a vehicle or street car shall drive the same
at a careful and prudent speed not greater than is reasonable and proper
having due regard for the traffic, surface and width of the street and

Fraudulent Indictment Pg 1

(b) Accused did drive and operate said automobile along and upon said Peachtree Street, while under the influence of intoxicating liquor, in violation of the law of Georgia;

(c) Accused did drive and operate said automobile along and upon said Peachtree Street at said intersection, and did fail to yield the right-of-way to the said Mrs John Marsh who was then and there a pedestrian crossing the roadway upon which accused was traveling at said intersection, the said Mrs Marsh crossing said roadway at the end of a block in an un-marked crosswalk, the movement of traffic not being regulated by a police officer nor by a traffic control signal, and there being no pedestrian tunnel nor overhead crossing provided at said intersection for the use of pedestrians, in violation of the lawful ordinance of the City of Atlanta, Georgia, which provided as follows,

"Code of the City of Atlanta. Section 88-501 (a). PEDESTRIAN'S RIGHT OF WAY. The driver of any vehicle shall yield the right of way to a pedestrian crossing the roadway within any marked crosswalk, or within any unmarked crosswalk at the end of a block, except at intersections where the movement of traffic is being regulated by a police officer or traffic control signals, or at any point where a pedestrian tunnel or overhead crossing has been provided."

(d) Accused did drive and operate said automobile along and upon said Peachtree Street, and did drive upon the left side of said roadway, said street not being a one-way street, the accused not passing another vehicle at said time, and there being no obstruction in said street to make it impracticable for accused to drive upon the right half of said street, in violation of the lawful ordinance of the City of Atlanta, Georgia, which provided as follows:

"Code of the City of Atlanta, Section 88-708 (a). Unless impracticable on account of obstructions, or when passing another vehicle, operators shall drive upon the right half of the roadway at all times. This provision shall not apply upon one way streets."

And as a result of the above described unlawful manner of operating said automobile, accused did with said automobile strike and hit and run against the said Mrs John Marsh, causing injuries, wounds and bruises upon her person from which she died; all of the said acts of accused being done without due caution and circumspection, and being contrary to the laws of said State, the good order, peace and dignity thereof.

Paul Webb, Solicitor General.
Special Presentment.

-2-

Fraudulent Indictment pg.2

138

DAD IN PRISON

From August 11,1949, until his death April 15,1994, my dad never felt free, he said there are different kinds of prison's, some don't have bar's and razor wire.

The prison he was in for forty-five years was a prison of secret's that he had to use for self protection from the State of Georgia that had used false evidence to get him indicted for crimes he didn't commit, and a vicious media that wanted him to suffer the worst punishment possible.

I asked dad how he felt his first day in prison, and his answer surprised me, he said he felt relief from some of the stress of being charged with murder, and being threatened with the death penalty if Margaret Mitchell died, along with all the other horrors he experienced after the incident happened. He said being away from people for a while was what he needed to feel safe.

He told me he was terrified when the Atlanta Police, and Bellwood Prison Camp put him in isolation away from other prisoners to keep him from being killed.

They kept him in protective custody the entire time he was in prison. He said it was mind boggling to know his only crime was being in the wrong place at the wrong time, and as a result he was in prison, with his life being threatened.

When the Fulton County Court acting on behalf of the State of Georgia found him guilty of involuntary manslaughter, he felt some relief that they didn't follow through with the murder charge they started with. He said the twelve to eighteen months in prison was much better than the "electrocution" the police "threatened" him with if Margaret Mitchell died.

He said he still felt like his life as he had known it was over, and would never be the same again; he was a changed man when he was released. Going to prison was something he never expected to happen to him in his lifetime, and when it was happening to him it was a shock to his system, and he was not sure he could withstand it.

He had only been married to his second wife Sybil for four months and he was concerned about how she and his four year old stepson Jimmy would survive without him to take care of them, he knew he couldn't keep his promise to his friend Jack Ross from a prison cell.

All he could think of that first night at the Bellwood Prison Camp was his sentence, and how he could survive it. He was isolated from the other prisoners for his personal safety therefore; he didn't have anyone to talk with to distract him from thinking about the recent events in his life, and how he would deal with them.

The past few months had been so chaotic he was ready for some solitude. He didn't think there could ever be anything "good" about going to prison however; he found that it was the best thing that could have happened to him at that time it forced him to think about everything without the tremendous stress he suffered immediately after the incident, and through the trial.

After his conviction, and prior to him going to prison everything was crazy, and mixed up, and he couldn't make sense of anything. After he arrived at the prison, and had a few days to calm down, and think about everything that was when everything started to make sense to him.

His wife bought all of the newspapers, and kept up with everything being said publicly, and that was published about the incident, then discussed it with him causing him to replay the incident repeatedly in his mind until he realized what was wrong with the story the police and the newspapers were saying that sounded ridiculous to him.

He was finally able to let everything that had happened sink in. That was when he decided that what had actually happened to Margaret Mitchell on August 11, 1949, would have to be known only to him, until the time was right to tell his story to someone that could tell the world he was not the person responsible for her death.

He knew that to do otherwise would be disastrous for him, and his family. He also knew that his time in prison would not be easy, especially with the burden he would have to carry for the remainder of his life.

The Warden at the Bellwood Prison camp talked to him about why he was there, and asked him about any concerns he had about his stay there. Dad told him about his ulcerated stomach problem, and that he would not be able to eat prison food without having severe health issues, and getting sick.

The warden said he had previously talked to the guards about him, and his situation, and all of them thought he had been treated unfairly, and they didn't think he should be there in the first place. The warden and prison guards reaction to him was a godsend for him at a time in his life that he desperately needed a miracle.

The warden and the guards had a makeshift kitchen set up where they cooked their food separate from the inmates and for helping to cook the food and keeping the wardens office area clean they let him share their food that probably saved his life.

He knew he couldn't survive on the kind of food the prisoner's were fed. That consisted of green's, dried beans, and cornbread that would have had a devastating effect on his stomach.

It also kept him busy, and made the time go by more quickly. He continued to analyze the facts in his case until he was convinced he knew without a doubt who was responsible for the death of "Margaret Mitchell", and it was not "Hugh Gravitt".

Dad told me many years later that if anyone with any common sense had ever looked at the facts in his case they would have realized she was not running backwards that she had to be falling backwards when her head hit his bumper.

After he got to the prison he thought about the nightmare he had been through for the past few months' and he knew he couldn't trust anyone on the outside to take his word for anything. He knew no one would believe him.

He said if John Marsh had enough power in Atlanta to kill his wife, and get someone else convicted, and sent to prison for it, without anyone questioning his participation in her death, he had the power to make sure anything he could say would be ignored as if he had never spoken.

John Marsh had the police, and the media convinced he was an invalid unable to shove his wife in front of a car, even though it was public knowledge that they frequently jaywalked on Atlanta streets weaving in and out of heavy traffic.

It was something he thought any intelligent person would know couldn't be done by someone too physically impaired to shove his wife under a moving car, and nothing dad could ever tell them would make any difference he realized for that reason, and others he couldn't tell anyone John Marsh killed his wife.

That was when he made the decision to keep his silence until the time was right to tell what actually happened to her and that time didn't come until he knew he didn't have long to live and that was when he told me everything.

The time he spent in prison was a turning point for him, he had to accept what had happened and learn to live with the stigma of the social unacceptability from everyone in the entire world who were familiar with "Gone With the Wind" and Margaret Mitchell who believed he was responsible for her death

The shame and disgrace he felt from going to prison was almost more than he could bear. It made him feel like he was nothing. He said it was very hard to accept the blame for taking a life, when he knew in his heart he was innocent.

He said what the police were saying, and what some newspapers were printing for public consumption was lies, and didn't closely resemble what had actually happened. Dad said he was shocked at how far they went to lie and distort the facts.

While he was in prison, my mother and stepfather discussed him adopting us. When they asked me what I thought about it, and explained to me that adoption would remove the stigma of the Gravitt name, and would change our lives.

I told them absolutely not. I can't imagine why they thought I would go along with what I considered such a ridiculous idea. I immediately wrote dad a letter and told him what they were suggesting.

I knew I wouldn't have a voice in the matter, and the only person who could stop it was him. The next few weeks were an unhappy time for me. Waiting for that answer from dad was very hard for me.

My dad was in prison, and my mother and the stepfather I hated were telling me that if they could get dad to agree to it Ralph would adopt Betty and me. They tried to make me believe that our life would be improved if we were adopted, and our name changed.

I was a child, and didn't know how the law worked in that kind of case. The only thing I could do at that point was to pray dad wouldn't go along with their plan, and thank god he stopped them in their tracks before it went any further. I never heard anything more about adoption.

Forty-three years later when dad and I were talking about the past, it came up, and I asked him why he didn't go along with their plans to adopt us. He said it was never an option as far as he was concerned.

He said he had done many stupid things in his lifetime however, that was never a mistake he would have made. He said when I wrote and told him what they had in mind, he got a message to mother, and put a stop to their plans, and the subject of adoption never came up to him again.

DAD AFTER PRISON

When dad came home from prison he was a changed man. He had always had an assertive personality, with confidence in himself to succeed at whatever he tried to do.

Then the hell he went through after the death of Margaret Mitchell, and the time he spent in prison he became quiet, and distrustful of people refusing to discuss the incident that had almost destroyed him with anyone. He took care of business, but made very few friends.

When dad came home Sybil was waiting for him, and they picked up where they left off ten months and twenty days earlier. They had only been married four months before the incident when Margaret

Mitchell was killed; nevertheless, he had already realized the marriage was in trouble before he went to prison.

My dad was very perceptive when someone was trying to put something over on him. Although he may have been lacking in formal education however; he did recognize obvious lies when he heard them, and especially when he heard from several of his friends who had seen her around town with different men while he was in prison, that made living with her difficult for him.

He knew he would have to wait until the time was right to end it, he had to get back on his feet financially, and this was not the right time for him to end the relationship. He said that going back to her and trying to make the marriage work after the separation was a huge mistake.

So much had happened that both of them had changed. He said he knew he should have started a new life immediately; however, she was not the kind of woman to let things go that easily.

The next thing he knew she was pregnant with Diane who is his third child, and he was on a roller-coaster that would last for almost two more years. He said he knew his father would turn over in his grave if he knew he was on the verge of another divorce, with a child involved.

He said the only thing about the divorce was that this one was not entirely his fault. We discussed it, and he explained what had happened when he and my mother got a divorce that "was his fault" he told me the same thing my mother and grandmother said happened, and I told him I didn't blame my mother that I would have done the same thing she did considering his record with women.

He knew deep in his heart that marrying Sybil Ross to keep a promise to a dying man was not a good enough excuse for marriage however; he had done it anyway to his own disadvantage.

While he was in prison he realized he had made a mess of his life that he thought would take a miracle to fix, and that miracle never materialized. He apparently had learned his lesson about women his next relationship lasted for thirty seven years.

My mother and her husband were having marital problems at that time, causing my sister and me to have to live with dad temporarily. It wasn't a good time for dad and Sybil to bring us into their home unexpectedly.

At that time, Diane was just a baby, and she was like a live baby doll to us, we loved playing with her, although our being there caused friction between dad and his wife, who was accustomed to having the freedom to do what she wanted while he was at work.

He always worked long hard hours, and it was usually between 9:30 pm, and 10: pm when he got home at night, Sybil would tell us to stay outside after dad came home to give them some privacy and she would let us know when we could come inside.

We had not lived with dad since we were very young therefore; we didn't know what his reaction to us staying outside in the street especially on school nights would have been.

We soon found out what he thought about it, and we were shocked. We didn't know at first that dad wasn't aware of the reason we were acting the way we did when he was at home.

We didn't understand enough about the kind of man he was to know that he would never agree for us to stay out on the street until 11: pm on school nights, or any other night.

The neighbor kids told their parents our situation and they let them stay outside with us until they had to go in and get ready for bed. Dad finally confronted us about it accusing us, thinking we were somehow wild and wanted to hang out in the street at night.

Even after he confronted us about it, we didn't tell him Sybil had told us to stay outside; we took the blame for it to keep her from getting in trouble with him.

We also didn't tell him about all the days she wasn't there when we came home from school. That she would come in just before time for him to get home, and take cold baths to clean up and try to sober up before he got there.

We could smell alcohol on her, and sometimes she would leave Diane, and her son Jimmy with her mother overnight. I don't remember how long this continued however, it came to a head when on a hot summer day she was ironing in the living room of the apartment with the front door open.

She was obviously mad at the world for reasons unknown to us when Betty who had been skating on the sidewalk came inside pulled her skates off, and left them on the living room floor.

The baby was fretful and crying causing her mother to scream at her to "shut up" she picked her up screaming in her face, and shook her furiously, then she put her back down on the floor. Betty picked the baby up to comfort her, when she did Sybil picked up one of the heavy metal skates off of the floor and threw it at her barely missing both of them, it went out the open door, and hit the door to the apartment across the hall, making a terribly loud sound.

She threw that skate hard enough if it had hit them they could have been seriously hurt. When this happened I looked at Sybil with a look that said you have made a "fatal mistake" then I ran out and went around to the back of the apartment building and came in the back door, I sat down on the steps that went up to the second floor picking a location where I could hear dad come in, and settled in for a long wait.

Sybil frantically searched the neighborhood telling Betty she had to get me in the house and talk to me before dad got home. She knew that if I told him what had happened, and told him everything she had been doing, she knew he would leave her and get a divorce. I sat there for what seemed like hours, and it probably was several hours waiting for him to come home.

While I waited, I thought about all of the times she had done things that I knew dad would forbid her to do. I thought about everything I was going to tell him, where I would have it straight in my mind before he came home. I could only hope that he would believe me when I told him what she had been doing ever since we came there to live.

I didn't know whether he would believe me, or if he would believe the lies she had been telling him for months. I only knew he needed to know about the skate incident that could have caused Betty and Diane to be hurt. He also needed to know that she had told us to stay outside when he was at home to give them privacy.

When he came in the front, I came in the back door. She had him around the neck crying hysterically, trying to make him think she was upset because I was missing when what she was actually afraid of was what I was going to tell him. She was telling him she didn't know where I was, that I had run out of the house, and she couldn't find me.

I waited for her to tell him everything she wanted to say, when she finished I said dad, she told you her story, now I am going to tell you mine. I told him everything she had been doing since Betty and I came to live with them while she stood looking at us listening, and crying.

Dad left her that night, and never lived with her another day. As a matter of fact I never saw her again. He got a divorce from her, she got custody of Diane, and he paid child support for her until she came of age.

Although I know I told dad the truth, I have always felt responsible for the breakup, and divorce that caused Diane to grow up without our father.

I truly believe that if my dad had stayed in the relationship with Sybil it could have ended tragically for him. If he had caught her in a compromising situation such as the one her next husband caught her in, I know it would have been disastrous.

After her marriage to dad ended, and he had divorced her, she got married again to a lab technician that worked in a metro Atlanta hospital, a marriage that went through a terrible example of what I feared my dad would have to go through if he ever found out first hand what kind of woman she was.

Dad said her husband told him that he suspected she was cheating on him therefore, one day he pretended to go to work then returned home unexpectedly, and found a man laying on their bed he shot the man, and killed him.

When the police came, they asked him to go down to the police station, where they let him go without charging him with murder, or anything else. Dad said he was glad he got away from her before something of that nature happened to him. He said he probably wouldn't have been as lucky as her husband was in not being charged with murder.

When dad went to see about Diane after he heard what had happened, Sybil's husband told him all about it. He also told him he was not going to divorce her over it that she wasn't going to get off that easily, that she was going to live with him for the rest of his life whether she liked it or not. If he knew at that time that he was terminally ill, he didn't tell dad.

As far as I know she did live with him until his death a few years later. I don't know if she ever got married again after he died, the subject didn't come up when Diane and her husband who live in Virginia came to visit dad before he got sick.

It had been a long time since he had seen her, and he was thrilled that she came to see him, and I'm sure she didn't want to discuss the past. I was glad he got to spend that time with Diane before he became too ill to remember that she had been there.

I was also happy to see her for the first time since she was a young child. She came back while dad was in the hospital, and was there to attend his funeral. Her mother Sybil was sick at the same time dad was, and they died within days of each other.

Dad never talked very much to me about Diane. All he ever told me was that he saw her occasionally while she was growing up. I do know that his relationship with her mother was contentious after the divorce causing him to avoid her as much as he could, and that probably kept him from having more of a relationship with Diane.

He said, she was the only good thing that came out of his marriage to Sybil and he loved her very much and that if he had ended the relationship with her mother before he went to prison she would have never been born, therefore, he was glad it worked out the way it did. He was glad he had her she was an important part of his life. He said having her made up for all the turmoil he went through with her mother.

Considering that dad had very little education, and with all the traumatic events he had to contend with he did very well for himself after his prison sentence ended in 1951, he owned his own business.

He learned enough working in the Service Department of the Veteran Cab Company to buy and operate his own service station with the assistance of an accountant to keep books for him. Fortunately when he left that job he never worked for anyone else as long as he lived.

Everything he did after leaving the Veteran Cab Company, and went into business for himself was moderately successful. He knew he could never drive a cab again therefore, he decided the best thing for him was to go into business for himself, and it worked for more than forty years.

In 1967 he bought twenty acres, and a house in Newton County near Covington Georgia, and sold his home in Dekalb County and moved his family to Covington.

He lived in the house that was on the newly purchased property, then he bought another house, and had it moved onto the foundation he had built, then he completely re-modeled it inside and used white brick on the outside. It made a very nice home for him and his family, where he lived until I moved him in with me.

Later on he bought another parcel of land where he built a service station, and started a landscaping business.

Dad's Third Marriage

After his divorce from Sybil, it was not long before he had wife number three. Her name was Dorothy Staton. They were together for thirty-seven years; they had three children together, Hugh Jr. Darlene, and Susan.

Dorothy was in her late teens when they got together, and she was that passive woman he had been looking for all of his adult life, she was somewhat like his mother, and from what he told me about their relationship, he was happy with her for most of those years. He said if she hadn't decided to go to work against his wishes he would have never divorced her.

She always knew where he was, and what he was doing. He said she always seemed to understand that there were issues he wouldn't discuss with her, or anyone else, and she never pressured him about anything. She was only three years older than I was, and I think he was like a father figure to her.

He said she was a tremendous help to him after they moved to Covington, at a time when he was struggling to build his business. She would go to the auto parts store for him, and run other errands that he couldn't take care of himself.

He said she would stay at the station when he had to be away for any reason, that kept him from having to have a paid employee, that he had to use at times, until he would catch them stealing from him.

From 1987, when he and Dorothy got a divorce, until 1991, when I moved to Covington to take care of him except for breakfast, he was living on Little Debbie Cakes, and other sweets. I feel certain that a diet of mostly sugar fed the cancer causing it to accelerate.

Dad hated being alone with no one to talk to, after all those years of hard work, when he didn't have time for idle conversation, now that he had the time he wanted someone with him all the time to talk with.

He thought his marriage to Dorothy was forever until she went to work and demanded her independence from him. That was when he decided to divorce her. When I learned about it I was very surprised. That was something I never expected to happen.

He said he was as happy with her as he could have been with any woman after the tragedy that consumed his life for more than four decades. He was a workaholic whose work helped keep his mind occupied, and he thought his life with Dorothy was secure, until she decided to find a job, and go to work.

He worked seven days a week most of their married life, something he could not have done with just any woman. It took a very special person, one that let him do what he needed to do, without becoming a quarrelsome nag.

I don't think he ever considered that she might have wanted more out of life than to sit at home with the children while he worked, and she wasn't the kind of woman to speak up and tell him what she needed that didn't include him.

After the early 1960s, I wasn't in close contact with dad, and his family for about twenty years, while he and Dorothy were raising their children, except through occasional phone calls, that were long distance, and usually short therefore, I never got close to their children, as a matter of fact today we barely know each other.

All I know about that part of his life is what dad told me after he and his wife were divorced, he was not on good terms with their children. He said their relationship worked as long as the children were at home and needed her, afterward is when she became restless, and started thinking about going outside the home to work.

He said their trouble began when she started earning her own money becoming independent from him making him feel she no longer needed, or wanted him. Dad was a man who didn't think a woman should work unless it was necessary for the family to survive.

He was from the old school that thought a woman's place was in the home. He didn't see her going to work as a necessity. He thought his income was sufficient to supply what they needed.

After he moved to Covington in 1967, he lived a much less stress-filled life that allowed his stomach problems to get much better, although they never completely went away. If he had quit smoking at that time, he could have overcome many of his physical problems. Dad just couldn't give up cigarettes, he said it was the hardest thing he had ever tried to do.

My dad was five ten, and he was very thin making him look taller than he actually was. His weight stayed at 140 to 150 pounds. He got up to 160 pounds once in his life, and that was when he quit smoking temporarily after being hospitalized where smoking was not allowed.

The last ten years of his life he was in very poor health, he had glaucoma that required him to use drops in his eyes every day to keep from going completely blind. His eye problems just about drove him out of his mind. He hated not being able to see as well as he once did.

He had already lost his sight completely in one eye before he found out he had glaucoma. His eyes were what bothered him more than anything. He had to have surgery in the 1980s because of circulation problems in one of his legs to stop the terrible pain.

Shortly thereafter, he had to retire from the heavy workload; he carried most of his life. He was never happy after he had to give up his business, and he could no longer go to work. He just seemed to give up on life, and started talking about dying soon, and that he couldn't die yet because he had unfinished business to take care of.

After I moved to Covington, and we spent time talking about his past he seemed to settle down, and became much calmer and at ease with everything.

I think before I moved there he was afraid he would die before he could resolve some issues he needed to address for his personal satisfaction that he had been living with for many years. He had a burden he needed relief from, and he knew I would help him with it if I possibly could.

Before he retired he found out he had spots on his lungs. However, he still refused to quit smoking, although his doctor told him how serious it was and, if he didn't quit he would eventually die from lung cancer.

His reply to the doctor was "I had to give up everything else, I will not give up my cigarettes" unfortunately that decision cost him his life. When his health deteriorated to the point that he knew he could never work again it took him a while to adjust to retired living. He never stopped thinking about how wonderful it would be to become strong enough to return to a job.

All of his life "work" had been his salvation. It had allowed him to survive circumstances that would have destroyed someone who didn't have his determination and endurance, as well as the ability to adjust to most any situation that came along.

He said the way he coped with stress was to get lost in whatever he was doing where he didn't have to think about what was happening in the present, and he could forget about the past temporarily.

I suspect that was one way he dealt with us ungrateful children, he would just continue on, and refuse to deal with the issues whatever they might be. It also made it impossible for him to establish close relationships with any of us, especially with his younger children, who grew up with parents who were complete opposites in every way. Dad was strong willed and authoritative, their mother was passive and easy going.

I suspect the dynamics of that household caused a lot of chaos in the home. That was probably why before he died some of his children had been alienated from him for years. His only son didn't attend his funeral.

He said he knew he hadn't been a good father in the sense of spending time with his children, he said he had never had the free time he would have needed to establish a close relationship with any of us, even the ones who lived with him. He said he had always had to work long hard hours to provide the kind of life he tried to give them.

He said his relationship with his younger children was more strained than with the older ones. He provided for them financially, but he had left them in the care of their mother for almost everything else.

She would tell him when they needed discipline making him the one who was responsible for any punishment needed. Therefore, his relationship with them was mostly in an area that could only breed resentment.

He devoted most of his time to his work. He said his family had suffered because of his failure to communicate in a way that was acceptable to them. Some of his children were not on friendly terms with him, and he didn't think he would ever be able to correct the mistakes he made with them.

He said all he could do now was to try to explain what had caused him to be the man he had become after 1949, although it was years before some of his children were born they couldn't imagine him before he went to prison. That man was barely visible by the time they were born.

I remembered all of it, and I told him he didn't have to explain anything to me that there had never been any doubt in my mind why he buried himself in his work, and shut everything else out for all those years.

I told him I never expected anything from him except his love, and I always knew he loved me. I think Diane was the only other sibling that felt the same way about dad that I did at least that was the impression I got from her when she came to visit him before he died.

He said the younger children didn't understand why he was so strict with them. He said the reason was that he didn't want them to make the same mistakes with their lives that he had made with his, and the other was his upbringing where his parents instilled in him that you do what "I say" not what "I do" and never talk back.

I think he came across to them as cold, and indifferent. He said, they thought he could have been more involved in their lives if that had been what he wanted, they saw it as his personal choice to let their mother raise them.

Whatever it was there were hurt feelings, and his life ended with the feeling that he had not been a good father to his children. Dad was different from most parents in our world today.

He didn't bend easily, when he said something, you could believe he meant it. He was that much like his own father. I always knew when he told me something I better listen and do what he told me. I never had a problem with that from him.

Sometimes children no matter what a parent does, or fails to do, their children never understand why their relationship with them doesn't work, and they go an entire lifetime without ever figuring it out.

What happened between dad, and his children was a clashing of wills, where there was no compromise, and that is a no win situation for either side. He thought his younger children would never understand him.

He asked me if I felt resentment toward him because he didn't play a more prominent role in my life. I told him that I never resented, or felt animosity toward him, that I had always loved him unconditionally, although I had also always felt the need to defend him.

He wanted to know if there was ever any happy or pleasant times in our lives, I told him there were some times when things were good when we were growing up although they were few and far between. Growing up in an environment of violence, and alcoholism can never be very pleasant.

There definately were times when I felt reasonably comfortable with my life such as it was. I guess when I realized there was nothing I could do to change my situation I just accepted it and moved on. I told dad not to worry about the past that we were going to make the future brighter for both of us.

Dad Talks about Murder

In 1991, he started telling me about the incident when he hit Margaret Mitchell, it was fascinating to me to learn how much he remembered about the incident that changed his life so drastically from the minute it happened, to the arrest, indictment, trial, and imprisonment.

He remembered even the smallest detail of it, every second from the time he saw Margaret Mitchell, and John Marsh standing in the middle of the street until he hit her, and afterward. I am aware that no one other than you can tell my story, because no one knows as much of my history as you will know when I'm finished.

I have never told anyone what I'm going to tell you, and I expect you to tell everything we talk about in the book I want you to write after my death that will let people know there is a side of this story that I could never bring myself to tell, and that they have never heard.

He said there are some powerful people in Atlanta that never want what actually happened to Margaret Mitchell to be told, People who made sure that I was aware of the power that was behind their intentional failure to inform the public that Margaret Mitchell and John Marsh were "jaywalking" and she was "drunk" when I hit her, and as a result she died.

Both Attorney and Gower told him that they had received personal threats because they they were representing him, serious threats that made them uneasy for numerous reasons the least of which was his innocence.

That was when they advised him not to ever talk about her death, that it would be best if he just forgot about what happened for his own good. They told him if he were to ever tell anyone the truth about her death he would be in more trouble than he could handle.

He said that at the time they told him not to talk about her death was before his trial, then they repeated it to him after he was convicted. They led him to believe that something awful would happen to him if he ever told anyone what he knew about the death of Margaret Mitchell.

When dad told me what his lawyer's had done to scare him out of talking about Margaret Mitchell being drunk and Jaywalking they were probably more interested in their own skin, and their family than they were that he would be convicted and go to prison.

They were not afraid dad would file ineffective assistance of counsel against them for not using the evidence they had in their possession to defend him, they were more afraid for the lives of themselves, and their family.

It was obvious to him that the Atlanta Police Department, Traffic Judge Luke Arnold, Prosecutor Paul Webb, the Georgia Court, and newspapers covered up the facts in the case because she was a rich and famous author and he was a lowly taxicab driver that they could easily sacrifice. They had used the personal threats against his lawyers to get them to throw him under the bus, and convict him.

Dad said Prosecutor Paul Webb made up lies to get a conviction when he saw they didn't have a legitimate case against him, and they were being pressured by everyone from President Truman, the Governor of Georgia, newspapers and the public to charge him with "murder".

As I listened to him tell what actually happened to her I realized it was something that no one had ever heard before. He knew "how" it happened, and that it wouldn't be an easy task for me to find the answer to "why" a middle aged overweight intoxicated woman would find herself in the middle of the block jaywalking on busy Peachtree Street in Atlanta Georgia endangering her life.

It was as if he had made an intentional effort never to forget anything about it. He knew it was important not to delay telling me everything he wanted me to know and as it turned out the three years, he spent telling me his life story was important. If he had waited longer he might not have been able to do it, and that would have been a tragedy in itself.

The worst thing about it was that he knew his health was deteriorating at a rapid pace, and that may explain why he considered it urgent for me to move near him where he could tell me what he wanted me to know about the death of Margaret Mitchell before it was too late, and he wouldn't be able to tell me that her death was not a result of an "accident" that it became "murder" when her husband John Marsh shoved her backwards into his car.

John Marsh really killed two people that day. My dad didn't die for forty-five years however, living with the burden of knowing "how" she died, and that he couldn't tell anyone, killed him slowly by degrees.

While he was telling me what actually happened to her tears flowed, and he was shaking uncontrollably, it was as if it was happening all over again in his mind.

It was startling and shocking to hear, and it took a minute for me to realize the magnitude of the bomb he had just dropped on me. The first thing I asked myself was how am I going to handle this?

The tremendous burden it had been for him to know the truth, then to realize he couldn't talk about it without re-opening the horror he had already suffered through once before, had just landed on me.

Now it had become my responsibility, and how could I handle it, unless I did the same thing he had done, and keep my silence which I have done for the past twenty years.

The feeling I was having at that time was that what dad had known for the past forty plus years was now my responsibility, but how does one handle knowing about a "murder" and to know you can't talk about it.

The first thing that comes to my mind is self preservation. Keeping silent had taken its toll on him, and it would probably do the same thing to me if I let it.

Dad said that immediately after Margaret Mitchell died his life began to be threatened by people the police took seriously enough that they put him in protective custody.

When he was transferred from the Fulton County Jail to the prison the protective custody was carried over into the prison where he was isolated from other prisoner's for the entire ten months and twenty days he was imprisoned.

Everything I have had to do over the past twenty years that would allow me to write this book has kept me going remembering what he told me, and the look on his face when he told me was an image I will carry to my grave.

The last year before dad died I spent reading about what he and I were discussing at the time concerning the book he wanted me to write, thinking about what made Margaret and John the kind of people they were that caused the turmoil in their lives.

It was a learning experience for me and helped me know that one day I would be able to keep the promise I made to my dad to reveal the truth about Margaret Mitchell's death when the time was right.

He said I know I don't have a lot of time left, and what I'm telling you is the most important thing I have ever told anyone in my life. He said he had waited all of those years before he was ready to tell anyone what had actually happened to her for a reason.

He said he had always wanted to tell his story where everyone all over the world would know the truth about how she died however; the right time never presented itself until now that his life was coming to an end.

When my dad asked me if I would write a book after his death, and tell his side of the incident that killed Margaret Mitchell I wasn't sure I was up to the challenge that would be involved. It took a lot of reading and researching subjects I didn't know anything about to convince me I could do it. He said he could tell me "how" she was killed, but I would have to find out "why". He said I would have to find out everything possible about her, and her husband John Marsh. He thought control of the money, their relationship, and the book they wrote was the key to why she was killed.

One of the first things he told me when we started to talk about Margaret Mitchell was "don't call it an accident" it was not an accident; from this time forward I want you to call it an incident.

At first I didn't understand why the distinction between accident, and incident, was important to him, until I looked the two words up, and learned the definition of an accident is something that happens by chance, without planning or intent. An incident is an event. He was right it was an incident.

Over the years in reading about her without talking about it to dad I concluded from what I read that she didn't die from trying to keep him from hitting her, that considering her lifelong problem with depression, and how unhappy she was, I thought it was possible that she had committed suicide, or that she deliberately ran in front of his car. He quickly discounted that theory.

When I suggested suicide to dad, he said you are way off track. "He said there was a lot more involved than a simple suicide" furthermore, after hearing his version of the incident, I understood why he never told anyone the truth about it.

He instinctively knew if he had ever told the police or anyone, what he knew had happened to Margaret Mitchell it would have caused even more chaos in his life, and the threats he continued to get for many years could have been carried out if he did anything that would shine a bad light on Margaret Mitchell or John Marsh.

He said what happened to her was terrible, and he knew if he told anyone they wouldn't have believed him. He said he didn't talk about it because he had never heard of anyone being killed in the way Margaret Mitchell's husband killed her, and he didn't think anyone would believe him. He said even until that day in 1991 he had never heard of a murder using "jaywalking", and a "moving car" to kill someone.

It was a nightmare dad never intended to confront again, even though his silence had allowed a murderer to go free. When I think about the impact Margaret Mitchell's death had on him it makes me feel both sad, and angry.

He was devastated over the fact that he had hit that woman with his car, and she died. Even though he knew her death had nothing to do with him, he had just been the "weapon available at the time used to kill her".

The reaction all over the world because she was the famous author of "Gone with the Wind" brought out the worst possible public hatred for my dad; it was cold, and unfeeling for the horrible nightmare, and suffering of another person unknown to them.

Anyone reading the newspapers would have thought he was an assassin hired to kill Margaret Mitchell when before that horrible incident he didn't even know who she was.

They made him out to be a monster, a cold-blooded killer, and he was far from being either of those things. He was a normal twenty-nine year old man who was on his way to a pharmacy to get medicine for his sick stepson. Never in his wildest dreams could he have foreseen what was about to happen to him.

He couldn't keep his thoughts straight enough to figure out what had happened until he went to prison where he was isolated away from the other prisoners to keep him safe. That isolation allowed him to think without the tremendous stress that he had been under since the incident occurred.

It was at that time when he was in prison that everything started to make sense to him. He began to replay the incident in his mind, finally realizing what was wrong with the picture being presented to the public by the police and the newspapers didn't come close to what actually happened to her, what they were saying and his wife was repeating sounded ridiculous to him.

After only a short period of time at the prison with no outside interferrence he was able to let, everything sink in. He started thinking about every aspect of the incident, and what he had actually seen.

At first when he realized that John Marsh had murdered his wife he didn't want to accept it. He kept telling himself that it couldn't have been what he saw. However; the more he thought about it, he realized that her "murder" was exactly what he saw, and that he had been made to take the blame for what her husband had done to her.

He said her husband had to have a motive for what he did, but not knowing anything about them he couldn't figure out why he would have wanted her to die, all he knew for sure was that her death was no accident.

He said later when he found out more about who she was and how rich and famous she was he thought the motive could have something to do with money, and her husband's manipulation that she would have fought tooth and nail until finally realizing she was in a no win situation.

He said what the Atlanta Police were saying, and the local newspapers were publishing for public consumption was lies, and didn't closely resemble what had actually happened. Dad said he was shocked at how far they went to lie about him and the cover-up of the facts by the police, the newspaper's the court and the powerful.

His mind went back to when he actually hit her, and he asked himself how she could have run "backwards" when he suddenly realized it is virtually impossible "to run backwards".

He knew there had been something strange surrounding the incident, and here it was, she was trying to catch herself after she had been "shoved" and in that split second, and the excitement of the moment it appeared to him that she was "running backwards".

He couldn't understand why she would go backwards toward traffic, instead of away from it. He repeatedly asked himself why she didn't go forward toward the theatre in the direction they had started where she would have been safe, and the answer to that question was that she "didn't run she was "shoved backwards".

Dad questioned why they were standing "dead still" in the middle of his lane of traffic, and when he moved over following the car in front of him, why they didn't continue in the direction of the curb toward the theatre where they were supposedly going.

His conclusion was that John Marsh had no intention of going to a movie; his intention was to "throw his intoxicated wife under a moving car".

The next day after the incident an article in the Atlanta Journal Newspaper on Friday August 12,1949, by Orville Gaines is a statement my dad made in which he stated exactly what happened when he hit Margaret Mitchell. This woman, he said had crossed the white center line in the street when a car passed her and she "started running backwards" I tried to miss her, but I just couldn't.

Dad said the key to this scenario is the way the police interpreted what he said immediately after the incident happened. That she was running "backwards" the police made it look like he said she was running back toward the curb where she had parked the car. "That was "not what he said".

Dad said the only thing he was absolutely sure of was that when he hit her she was not running, she was "falling backwards" her arms went up as if she was grabbing at him trying to catch herself, she couldn't catch herself, and fell hitting her head on my bumper.

He said it was as if someone had turned a light on in his mind when he realized she had not run backwards, that her husband had shoved her.

Then he said he remembered that they were not walking forward toward the theatre where her husband said they were going he couldn't understand why the police or the news media, or someone somewhere didn't question that.

They were standing still, facing each other, his back toward the curb on the side of the street toward the theatre. Dad's impression was that they were arguing, or waiting for something, instead of continuing across the street in the direction they had started.

After he had it, all figured out he knew what they were waiting for. John Marsh was keeping her distracted while the two cars he had seen at the Thirteenth Street intersection got close enough to them for the first car to go around, and then he shoved his wife backwards toward the second car, which was his car.

I said, dad do you know what everything you just told me actually means? His answer was "what do you think it means?" I told him I think John Marsh did kill his wife and he got away with it. He said "I know he did" there is no doubt in my mind about it, I've known what the truth was about her death since 1949, but I could never bring myself to talk about it.

Dad said there was no damage to his car. There was not even a scratch on It. The police kept that quiet, and no one ever mentioned the other car that was in front of him that had moved over, straddling the center white line to go around them.

He said it was also strange that Marsh had waited until it was dusky dark, and time for the next movie to start, when there would be people leaving the theatre causing more traffic at that time, and crossing in the middle of the block where there was no street light, a location where no one would expect pedestrians to cross, they wouldn't be seen.

He was accurate in that, no one saw them until they heard an inaudible scream that dad thought occurred at the moment her husband John Marsh gripped her before he shoved her backwards into his car.

The newspapers never mentioned the fact that there was two cars, or that the traffic was heavier that day than normal because of the well publicized movie at the Peachtree Arts Theatre.

I asked him why he never went to the police with the story he had just told me, and he said he didn't trust the Atlanta Police to do anything, and his lawyer's had cautioned him not to ever talk about what actually happened on Peachtree Street on August 11, 1949.

He said for them to tell the truth about how John had led his intoxicated wife into the middle of Peachtree Street where there was no crosswalk, and illegally jaywalk to her death making John responsible for her death was the only thing that could have helped him and he could never see that happening.

Neither the police, or John Marsh would ever have admitted the truth, and John never intended to take responsibility for anything related to her death.

She was dead, and nothing dad could do would bring her back. He knew it would have been detrimental to him if he told the police that John Marsh killed his wife he would have become a standing joke. And that would have been devastating to a man like him. His pride could not have withstood that kind of humiliation.

He said he thought the prosecutor and the police knew Marsh killed his wife, and because of who she was they didn't dare say anything that would have caused public sentiment against them they just covered it up.

Prosecutor Paul Webb used false evidence to get an indictment against him. The State of Georgia tried, convicted, and sentenced him to twelve to eighteen months in prison, and there wasn't anything anyone could do to fix that.

According to their friends, and people who knew their habits they regularly jaywalked in downtown Atlanta, and dad said he thought that was to get her accustomed to jaywalking where she wouldn't question it when the right time came to get rid of her. "Jaywalking and a fuzzy mind from champagne cocktails set the scene for the "perfect murder".

Then he said if you had been in my shoes, what would you have done? He said by the time he could think with a clear mind, to figure out what had actually happened they had found him guilty, and he was in prison, and there was no way the authorities were going to take a prisoners word for anything, especially a prisoner convicted of killing the famous author of "Gone with the Wind.

He said when I had it figured out; I knew my conclusion would be devastating to me if I tried to do anything about it. Can you imagine what would have happened if I had told, the police, or anyone that John Marsh killed his wife by shoving her in front of my car? The media would have had a field day at my expense they would have made me look like some kind of fool that was trying to put the blame on someone else.

He said there was nothing in the street between them and the curb toward the theatre to prevent them from continuing across the street if that had really been their destination, and if you consider that John Marsh had planned to kill her before that day, he would have picked a time when a special event was taking place in downtown Atlanta, to insure that there would be more than usual traffic, an event such as the well publicized Italian Movie showing at the Peachtree Arts Theatre.

Then he would have made sure she was intoxicated enough that she wouldn't question why they had parked where they would have to cross the street at a dangerous location to get to the theatre.

Dad said what happened to Margaret Mitchell was not a decision made on spur of the moment, it was a well thought out plan an almost "perfect crime" And when the opportunity presented itself he was ready for it. I said dad, he didn't almost commit the perfect crime, and get away with it, he did commit the perfect crime, and he did get away with it.

There was an inaudible scream heard by people leaving the theatre, that was probably when he gripped her, and she realized what he was about to do.

She had told a friend in 1945 that she was going to die in a car crash, that she felt certain of it. Her husband may have been threatening to kill her for years before he finally acted on it.

It makes me cringe to think about what must have been going through Margaret's mind at the moment he gripped her, and she knew what he was going to do to her, she had told friends she was going to die in a car accident, and that time had arrived. The only thing she could do was to scream although the people leaving the theatre who heard her scream could not make out what she said.

John Wanted Letter's Destroyed

When you think about what she told her friend Edwin Granberry that she felt certain she was going to die in a car crash, she didn't say "I think" or "I might" she said she felt "certain" of it. She also told her friend Granberry no matter who should ask him to do so "not to destroy her letters".

John Marsh was the only person that ever asked anyone to destroy her letters. According to her biographers immediately following her death John asked their secretary Margaret Baugh to contact everyone she had written, and ask that they destroy any correspondence from her.

That included his own family who refused to honor his request which is something that makes me wonder why they chose to keep her letter's regardless of the fact he asked them to destroy them.

It tells me his family knew something was wrong with his need to have all correspondence from her destroyed. I have to ask myself if their reasoning could have been that they knew the relationship between John and Margaret was not what everyone thought it was, and they feared they would be destroying evidence.

The only reason I can think of that he would have wanted to destroy all of her possessions was either to "erase her from existence", or he was afraid what she had written to her friends would incriminate him.

Was he afraid someone would look at the whole picture, and figure out that he had forcefully encouraged her to write the stories for the book, and after he retired he was stuck with a woman who was anything but pleasant to live with.

Her reaction to the way he treated her may explains why she suffered from a such a deep depression for years, that got progressively worse after 1944.

She was trapped with a man who had changed her life into what he wanted it to be, confirming Medora Perkerson's theory that his manipulation, and control was changing her, and had turned her into person obcessed with illness. Her only alternative to staying with him was to go back to her father's home, where her every move would have been monitored, and she had no intention of doing that.

I also wonder why the conversation with Granberry was not reported to the police when she actually died in the car crash that she had predicted, and warned him about. If he reported it to the police, why didn't that put the spotlight on John Marsh where it should have been from the beginning?

If no one were threatening her life, why would she tell her friend she felt certain she was going to die in a car crash? Could it have been coincidence? I don't think so.

Living in that apartment with her, and all of her ailments, with the knowledge that he couldn't escape her any other way. Dad said he thought that may have been why he killed her, and then he tried to erase her existence by destroying everything that defined her.

He started destroying her personal possessions along with the clothes she was wearing when she was hit on the day after her funeral. Everything he did after her death leads me to believe his actions were to destroy evidence, I don't think it had anything to do with what she wanted.

The only evidence I've been able to find that anyone questioned his actions when he destroyed the original manuscript of "Gone With the Wind", along with most of her personal papers was her Secretary Margaret Baugh who did question his bizarre actions.

Why would he try to hide something unless he thought he had something that needed to be kept secret, or covered up? My dad thought it was "murder: and a lot more".

Destroying the manuscript and all of her papers didn't prove she wrote the book, it would have done the complete opposite, and "should" have caused everyone who knew she didn't have the "education, or literary experience" that it took to write a book of that quality, and magnitude to demand answers.

Dad said, Margaret Mitchell, and "Gone With the Wind", are known all over the world, and people everywhere think I am a monster, and a killer, and they will continue to believe that, unless you tell them the truth.

He said he had thought about other aspects of the incident, and he thought a reasonable person would have known he wasn't driving as fast as the police, and the witnesses said he was. Apparently they didn't consider the heavy traffic in that area of Peachtree Street that night due to the popular movie playing at the Peachtree Arts Theatre.

He said the reported 67 feet of skid marks were more lies told by the police to make it look like he was going a lot faster than he was. Can you imagine the damage it would have done to his car and especially to her if he had been driving as fast as John said he was? He wanted everyone to believe dad hit her running at least 50 mph and there was very little blood, and no damage to her clothes.

Dad said the police estimated his speed at between 25 and 30 mph. John Marsh testified that if he were going less than 50 mph he would have been surprised. Another witness first said he was driving 50 mph, and then changed his speed to 40 mph, when 15 to 20 mph would have been more accurate.

Dad said there was heavier traffic on Peachtree Street that evening than was normal, and it would have been impossible for anyone to drive the speed the witnesses including John Marsh testified he was.

If a car weighing more than three thousand pounds going 50 mph were to hit a person who was standing upright as John Marsh testified she was, it would have caused her to go airborne for several feet, and there would have been blood, and damage to the car. There was neither, according to her death certificate the only injury Margaret Mitchell sustained was to her head, causing brain damage.

Marianne Walker one of her biographers wrote that John Marsh told his mother there was no damage to her clothes caused from the incident, there was no blood on them, and he said her face was not even dirty.

Those clothes were evidence, and I question why the police chose to ignore them allowing John Marsh to go to the hospital the day after her funeral to retrieve and immediately burn them along with the shoes she was wearing, without arousing suspicion from her brother, the police or anyone else.

That wasn't the only thing he burned, their maid Bessie, and her secretary talked about the numerous boxes of her belongings he burned that day. I just cannot wrap my mind around why a man who supposedly loved his wife would destroy her belongings immediately after her funeral, when he should have been mourning her death. It was something that should have raised suspician.

I think the fact that he immediately started destroying her belongings including her clothes and the shoes she was wearing when she was fatally injured tells a story of its own. I asked dad if his lawyer questioned John about why he felt the need to burn evidence before the police had a chance to look at it to determine what had really happened to her.

His answer was that John Marsh was never questioned in any way by the police or anyone else that could have determined his participation in his wife's death. He had escaped any kind of scrutiny, and to me that is unacceptable.

The newspapers lied when they said dad dragged her fifteen feet. The accident report does not show that he dragged her at all. However, after John Marsh burned her clothes and shoes there was no proof of that. Those items would have shown it if she had been dragged.

Her husband deliberately destroyed evidence that could have possibly implicated him in his wife's death. Why would he hurriedly destroy them after her death before anyone else thought about them, or could look at them?

The first police officer at the scene testified that dad looked and acted like someone in shock. I asked him about that, and he said he was in shock, and scared.

He said he was praying that she would recover although every instinct he had told him she had died August 11, not August 16, 1949. Dad said John Marsh didn't have a shocked look on his face, because he was not shocked at what had happened to his wife.

Dad couldn't understand how a man who had been married to a woman for all those years wouldn't feel something when she was lying in the street possibly dying. I answered him with "dad, you are not a psychopath" that is why you cannot understand how he reacted to her situation.

He said what do you think he would have done if I had told the police I saw him shove his wife in front of my car? I said "he wasn't worried about it one way or the other at that time. He knew the police wouldn't believe you no matter what you said."

That is another trait of a psychopath; he was so arrogant, and sure of himself that even though he had no way to know for sure what you saw, he just continued to play the victim.

I told dad that when the trial was over he must have felt complete confidence that he had been successful in killing his wife, and getting away with it.

So confident in fact that he thought no one would ever question his responsibility for her death because of her fame, and social standing in Atlanta, and because the man who happened to be driving the car that hit her was a taxicab driver with "no respect, or standing in the community".

His psychopathy allowed him to live in peace for the rest of his life, with no regret, or remorse. He could lie down at night, and sleep in peace never feeling guilt about his wife's death.

Dad said he couldn't imagine anyone who could be that cold hearted, and I told him he had witnessed the closest thing to a perfect murder that he would ever see, and he agreed.

There were many people in Atlanta who knew John Marsh, and how strange he was, why didn't anyone question the circumstances of her death? I will never believe that her brother didn't see anything suspicious concerning the unusual circumstances surrounding her death, and the manner in which she died. Especially after she had predicted that she would die in a car accident, and had asked her friends not to destroy her letters no matter who should ask them to perform such a bizarre task.

THE VICIOUS MEDIA

T he media continued to harass dad for many years after he got out of prison. They lost him for a few years after he moved to Covington. One day in 1991 while I was at work and dad was at home alone a reporter by the name of Gary Pomerantz from the Atlanta Journal Constitution Newspaper showed up while dad was sitting in the yard trying to relax.

Pomerantz with his recorder that he thought he had hidden under the pad he was going to take notes on thought he could fool dad, and that he wouldn't know he was recording his conversation.

He underestimated dad's power of observation when he was dealing with the media; he saw the recorder immediately although he didn't tell him at the time he had seen it. The newspaper received some negative input from letters to the editor after they published that article.

He started asking dad about the incident in 1949 when he had hit and fatally injured Margaret Mitchell, and dad told him clearly he didn't want to discuss Margaret Mitchell with him. Dad was a frail old man therefore; the reporter overrode his objections and proceeded to ask him personal questions refusing to adhere to his clear and emphatic "no I don't want to talk about Margaret Mitchell".

Instead of leaving when dad told him he didn't want to talk to him he just kept asking him about a subject he didn't want to discuss with him, until dad finally just gave up. He was very upset when I got there that afternoon; he said he felt completely helpless when that reporter kept insisting he tell him about Margaret Mitchell.

I get fighting mad when I think about the way the local newspapers degraded and trashed my dad for forty-five years. In 1991 when Gary Pomerantz came to dad's home, he was old, and he was not well, he didn't have the energy to fight it any more, therefore, his situation allowed the reporter whom I think was completely without conscience to take advantage of an old man when his defenses were down; it certainly was not a moral or ethical thing to do.

This was not an interview, it was another public insult, and the only one dad ever gave to my knowledge. I think the Atlanta Journal Constitution, and their reporter Gary Pomerantz was wrong to take advantage of him in that manner after he gave them an "emphatic no" to talking about Margaret Mitchell.

Just about everything online about Margaret Mitchells death falsely describes her being hit by a taxi-cab driven by a man who was drunk. The following article explains better than I can how the media has never stopped their onslaught of my dad even years after his death.

On April 21, 2010, the Observer in Winter Park Florida ran an article titled Wrongs, and Rights by Louis Roney that they posted on the internet, where he stated one evening in 1949, on a night off between performances as Lt. Pinkerton in Madam Butterfly with the Atlanta Opera Company, I went to see a highly touted Italian film in a small theatre on Peachtree Street in Atlanta. {"I don't know if he actually went to the movie, or if he just made that up the same way, he made up what he saw"}.

Louis Roney said when the movie was over, and he walked out of the movie theatre he saw a turbulent scene in front of him across Peachtree Street, he said police cars were everywhere, and an ambulance with sirens blasting was driving away from the scene.

He said a taxi stood slantwise in the street, the drivers' door open, front wheels against the curb. The police were holding the arms of a young man who was the taxi driver. Louis Roney lied about witnessing the arrest of my dad after he hit Margaret Mitchell. He lied when he said the car that hit her was a taxicab. {The movie was over at 8: pm the ambulance didn't leave the scene until almost 9: pm therefore, Roney wants his readers to believe he stayed at the theatre an hour after the movie ended}.

He said a hushed gasp dominoed through the crowd on the sidewalk. Its Margaret Mitchell he hit Margaret Mitchell He was driving that taxi there. He was driving like a bat out of hell Margaret Mitchell had gotten out of a car and started across Peachtree Street, she never saw the taxi coming. {My dad was not driving a taxicab when he hit her; he was driving his private car a 1949 Ford}.

Roney stated, Margaret Mitchell, author of Gone with the Wind, hung on to life through five agonizing days. Hugh Gravitt the twenty-nine year old taxi driver had killed one of the most beloved Georgian's who ever lived.

Gravitt stated that she had darted in front of his cab. My dad's statement was that she ran backwards and he couldn't miss her. He had tried to miss her but couldn't. Roney said the front page of the next days Journal-Constitution gave the tragic story the kind of space it had given to Pearl Harbor, and the death of Franklin Roosevelt.

He continued, letters to the editor screamed hysterically for retribution, that Gravitt should be tried for murder, and jailed for life, or executed. Gravitt was charged and convicted of involuntary manslaughter. He served about ten months in prison. He had not known Mitchell, nor had he intended to kill her. If his taxi had killed Jane Doe, the case might have been buried deep in the inner pages of the newspaper.

He said Hugh Gravitt died at 74 in Cumming Georgia. The cause of death was unannounced. Gravitt's life had been that of a recluse in the small Georgia town {"Another Roney lie". Dad had not lived in Cumming since the early 1940s, and he was never a recluse in Cumming, or anywhere else}.

I don't have any idea where Roney got his erroneous information; Dad had a job waiting for him in the Service Department of the Veteran Cab Company when he left prison. He also bought two cars and leased them to the cab company for extra income. He lived in Atlanta with his family, where he owned and operated several businesses until 1967.

He was right about one thing I kept his death, and funeral quiet, because I didn't want his last moments on this earth to turn into a media circus that he would have detested. Roney quoted dad as saying he had rather it had been him instead of her, and that he would have gladly taken her place.

Dad did say that, and he was serious about it, he would have gladly taken her place, even after he realized her death hadn't been what it appeared to be at first. His feelings about Margaret Mitchell were that she didn't deserve to die in such a violent way.

Then Roney said "I wonder if Gravitt ever heard prize fighter Joe Louis famous words. You can run, but you can't hide. My dad never ran from anything, or anyone. He continued to live a normal life in Atlanta Georgia until 1967. {Roney may have been right when he said that from 1949 onward everyone who heard the name Hugh Gravitt related it to the death of Margaret Mitchell}.

People like Louis Roney have never let him rest even these many years after his death they are still trying to crucify him, to make him look bad in the eyes of the public. Every year on the anniversary of her death, he would get phone calls from the media with questions such as "how does it feel to know you are a murderer? Those phone calls were pure torture for dad, and he despised the local newspapers, He said they didn't care about people.

They would call and pretend to be someone else until they got dad on the phone then they would say awful things to him before he could hang up the phone. That went on as long as his number was listed in the Atlanta telephone directory.

I called the Observer Newspaper that published the Louis Roney article, and the woman I talked to told Roney she had talked to me, and that I was upset about his article. He called me and tried to justify what he had said about dad, and that he was at the scene of the incident when dad hit Margaret Mitchell although nothing he said he saw closely resembled what actually happened.

I told him exactly what I thought about his article, and I didn't mince my words. I guess he was desperate to come up with a story that might get some public attention for him, and his newspaper. I was furious when I read it. However, just because he was old and blind it doesn't give him the right to keep up the media war on my dad's memory.

There are numerous internet sites who are still repeating all of the lies published in 1949 about her being hit by a drunken taxicab driver. "My dad was not drunk when he hit Margaret Mitchell" and the only thing I can do to right the wrong done to him is to write about it in this book and hope the truth will resignate with those that read it.

Winecoff Hotel Fire

The years from 1944, to 1949, were traumatic years for dad. His wife divorced him and took his children away; He almost died from ruptured ulcers that required a part of his stomach to be surgically removed. His best friend died after having brain surgery. He witnessed things that were beyond anything he could have imagined, until he saw it happening with his own eyes.

He had never interacted with law enforcement, for anything more than a traffic ticket, and he knew nothing about how the law works. The five years he lived in Atlanta prior to 1949, had shown him a picture of what hell was really like, nothing good ever seemed to happen for him there, it was like a magnet to him that he couldn't resist for many years.

Although everything in his personal life since my mother left him, and took us back to Forsyth County had been chaotic, his imagination could never have grasped the fact that he had a date with destiny on Peachtree Street on August 11, 1949, that would change his life forever.

The first public disaster he witnessed in Atlanta happened when he was driving a cab for the Yellow Cab Company and was at the home of his girlfriend who lived near the Winecoff Hotel.

All at once in the night, they heard sirens blasting loud enough to wake the dead. They went outside to see what was happening, and to their amazement the Winecoff Hotel was on fire, they got as close as they could and stay safe, then they watched as the fifteen stories of the Winecoff Luxury Hotel built in 1913, without sprinklers, fire escapes, or even a fire alarm system, burned killing one hundred nineteen people,

It was a scene etched in dad's memory for the rest of his life by the "horror" of watching people young and old leaping to their death. He saw mothers throwing their babies out windows to keep them from burning alive, before they followed them to their death to escape the smoke and fire.

He saw two young girls put their arms around each other, and jump to their death. He said it was the worst thing he had ever seen, and he talked about it often throughout the years. He said he, and his girlfriend, along with bystanders who were watching were in shock, with tears flowing, they were crying so hard their whole body's shook, but they could not bear to look away.

Dad said even the firefighters and emergency people who were desperately trying to save people couldn't do anything, because they didn't have ladders that reached high enough, and there was nothing they could do without the needed equipment to reach them. It was chaos for everyone including the firefighters who were helpless to save the guests in the hotel who were screaming as they jumped from windows on the upper floors where the fire fighters couldn't reach them.

Dad said even the firemen were crying so hard they were convulsing, and all they could do was watch in horror the worst mass suicide to escape the smoke, and fire that they had ever seen.

The last time I heard dad telling anyone about watching the Wincoff Hotel burn was when he was reminiscing about the past with Attorney John Degonia in Covington, Georgia while we waited for his will to be prepared. I don't know if Attorney Degonia knew he was talking to the man who had fatally injured Margaret Mitchell in 1949. If he recognized dad's name he didn't ask any questions about it.

I asked dad, why he could talk about the Winecoff burning, and he couldn't talk about Margaret Mitchell. He said in his mind there was a difference. He said he was a bystander at the Winecoff disaster-watching people die. Talking about Margaret Mitchell was too personal to him, and he never felt comfortable talking about her or the incident to anyone.

He said talking about her made him feel apprehensive afraid he would say too much before he was ready to tell what had actually happened to her.

He said if anyone ever questioned the circumstances of her death, or ever wondered if the published account was true he never heard about it. He said people everywhere have accepted the published accounts of her death and most likely will never believe anything else.

He said the police, and the newspapers just made up what they wanted it to be without looking at anything that would have helped him, such as jaywalking, and the fact that she was intoxicated when he hit her.

They never brought any of that to the attention of the public. Dad said his attorney knew and there is no way the police wasn't aware that she was drunk and jaywalking. The facts in this case have never been made public until now.

SHOCKING REVELATIONS

When dad and I started talking about Margaret
Mitchell and John Marsh, he told me that what I
needed to know in addition to what he was going
to tell me would have to come from the recorded history of her
relationship with her husband.

He said her death was not the result of a sudden impulse to go to
a movie, that what he saw when he hit her had taken careful thought,
and planning. My research on John Marsh confirmed that he was
capable of planning a perfect murder.

What I learned about them through reading about their relationship was that Margaret and John were very secretive about their personal life, because what they had was not a normal marriage where

two people get married for traditional reasons; neither of them was interested in the institution of marriage

Everything I read about them told me the basis of their relationship was the "bargain" they made to live together and write a book. Stephens Mitchell said his sister's secretiveness was not because she had something to hide however; I differ with his opinion, I think both Margaret and John had a quite lot to hide.

When I started researching for this book I wasn't interested in reading about how wonderful Margaret Mitchell and John Marsh were; I wanted to know the facts about them from their childhood until the day they died.

I wanted to know what made them tick, and in order to tell what kind of people they were, and what led him to eventually kill her made their upbringing important. The evil that killed Margaret Mitchell didn't happen overnight.

I was fascinated that two people whose outlook on life was totally different, and who had absolutely nothing in common except a definite distaste for marriage, and the opposite sex could, or would ever get married, especially to "each other" and stay married for twenty-four years before that marriage, and her life came to a violent end.

I was curious about how he managed to dominate, and control a woman who had never let anyone manipulate her, or tell her what to do. I wanted to know how he managed to destroy everything that made her the flamboyant self indulgent person she was, changing the very things she had fought her father, and her grandmother over to the bitter end, never giving in to them.

I wanted to know how he turned her into a depressed hermit that would let him control every aspect of her life, taking away all the fire and spirit she publicly exhibited before she met him. I read where she once made the statement that she and John knew secrets about each other that no one else knew.

I wonder if one of the secrets she knew about him had anything to do with the letter he wrote to his sister Frances in late March 1922, when he sent her a picture of Margaret and and Red Upshaw whom he described as one of Margaret's lovers and his roommate, that she might find interesting .

Then he said something I feel is quite telling, he said, "I could love one or the other if the other dear charmer were gone." This was a strange statement coming from John Marsh, it sounds las if and Red Upshaw may have been lovers.

I wonder why he would have written something like this to his sister unless his family, or at least his sister Francis was aware of his sexual preference.

Margaret was very secretive from the time she was a child about her personal life therefore; if she told John her lifelong secrets that she didn't want anyone else to know she would have been terrified after he showed her the real monster behind the mask, along with the possibility that he started to threaten her life after the book was published, and she cut him out of the negotiations for the movie rights.

Some may say these things are not related, but I will show you how from the time Margaret Mitchell met John Marsh in 1921, when my dad was only one year old, their lives were set on a path that led to her death, and to dad's imprisonment for crimes he never committed, and that have never to this day been investigated by reliable sources.

What dad told me happened to her gave me a better understanding of the relationship between her, and her husband that was very different from what everyone thought it was. Therefore, when I started analyzing what others had written about them I was shocked at what I discovered.

Based on her biographer's views, and there were many, it was obvious to me that everyone who wrote about her life had realized who, and what Margaret Mitchell, and John Marsh really were however; their written evaluation of them was different from mine.

Everything I read about them just seemed to jump off the page at me with a story that would lead me to research things I had never thought about before.

It was certainly not something I would have previously thought would relate to Margaret Mitchell, or her husband, such as sexual deviance, psychosomatic disorders, and psychopathic behavior all of which was attributable to both of them. It would take me through their lives from their childhood, until their death.

I told dad that their relationship was never a storybook love affair; it was a "bargain", made between two people to write a book, it was never about being in love, and living happily ever after, it was the opposite.

When I told him what I was learning about them he wasn't as surprised as I was, he said he knew there had to be a dark side to their relationship, or he wouldn't have killed her in the violent manner he did.

After I started reading about Margaret and John's bizarre illnesses, I found where renowned Psychiatrist Hervey Cleckley who was the author of Mask of Sanity published in 1941, diagnosed Scarlett O'Hara, as a partial psychopath, and when his book was published Margaret contacted him praising him for his diagnosis of Scarlett, and afterwards she became so ill she was bedridden for several weeks.

Margaret having known for most of her life that she wasn't normal, and that there was something seriously wrong with her, she had never been diagnosed by a Psychiatrist. Cleckley's diagnosis answered some of the questions she had about her own mental condition, and through Scarlett she could learn about herself, after all it didn't matter if she was called Peggy, Pansy, Scarlett, or Margaret they were all one and the same.

When I read Cleckley's diagnosis of Scarlett it was obvious to me that it also fit Margaret Mitchell perfectly. In his opinion Scarlett showed the emotional impoverishment of patients presented as partial psychopaths whose capacity for a true commitment in love could not be modified that she was selfish, and only interested in her own wants and needs. He sensed an inward hollowness, and a lack of insight in her.

John Marsh also exhibited some of the traits Psychiatrist Cleckly described as psychopathic traits in his unemotional reaction to his wife when she was lying in the street fatally injured, and possibly dying after being hit by my dad's car. He showed no understanding, or care for her pain and suffering.

He also exhibited the traits of the men described by Robert Hare in "Snakes In Suit's". He was cold and indifferent and his manipulation of Margaret Mitchell should have been obvious especially to those close to her should have realized he had an agenda, that was all about writing a book that had been his lifelong dream to go down in history as a man of literature.

I think human nature contradicts that a dedication with his initials in the book was all he wanted from it. After working on it for ten years under less than pleasant conditions I will never believe he would accept such a pittance of the fame and fortune she received from the book without some kind of retalliation.

Why her brother, or her father never questioned why he gave in so easily on something he was so obsessed with that would only make her rich and famous is beyond my comprehension.

John had made statements to his mother about moving back to Kentucky when he became a famous writer. The "bargain" he and Margaret made before their marriage turned into a disastrous tragedy with shocking consequences.

For them to live together she would have to give up her social life, and live a life of seclusion with him in a one-bedroom apartment in Atlanta Georgia where the summers are blistering hot, and they didn't have air conditioning while she wrote stories about the civil war, and the lives of people she knew, or was told about as a child on the laps of the old veterans of the Civil War and other relatives.

For those reading this book who may not know everything about Margaret Mitchell she was born on November 8, 1900 at 296 Cain Street in Atlanta Georgia, in a home owned by her grandmother Stephens. She had one brother her parents named Stephens taken from her mother's maiden name.

Her mother Maybelle Stephens Mitchell was an intelligent educated woman, and a dedicated women's rights advocate who was out of the home on trips for long periods leaving her children Stephens, and Margaret in the care of their father, and the servants.

Margaret grew up listening to her mother preach to women that they had a right to defy their husbands, and make decisions on their own, therefore, it isn't surprising that Margaret grew up with a negative attitude toward men, and motherhood.

Her father Eugene Mitchell was a busy man involved in his law practice, and other important project's he was involved with. It was a time when both parents were busy with their own interests.

They had very little time for their children, leaving them many times without constant supervision, unprotected from the dangers that can befall children in this situation. It seems Stephens survived it unharmed; I don't think the same can be said about his sister.

When Margaret was three years old her dress caught on fire from an open heating grate, and from the fear of that happening, again her mother stored her dresses away, and started dressing her in Stephen's clothes to prevent another such accident.

Dressing her as a boy caused the neighbors to tease her calling her "Jimmy", and the neighborhood children began to taunt her. This happened in her formative years, and was the first of her lifelong searches for her "identity".

Wearing pants and acting like a boy made her acceptable as a playmate for her brother, and his friends, who were a few years older than she was. She became a tomboy with a strong sense of adventure. She loved playing baseball, and other rough, and tumble boy games with her brother, and her new friends.

I'm not sure that was an acceptable lifestyle for a young girl, where she played with boys who were a few years older than she was, with more mature ideas and knowledge than she had. I don't know any parents of a young girl who would let their young female child play with older boys unsupervised, even if she did dress like a boy.

Her brother Stephens Mitchell said she never played with dolls. This could account for her lack of interest in feminine things and later not wanting to have children of her own, it was said that she didn't possess a motherly nurturing instinct.

On her first day of school she told her mother she didn't like school and didn't want to go back, her mother became so angry with her for her attitude about school, that she gave her a spanking with a hairbrush.

That was when she was told that without getting an education and preparing for the future she would have trouble making it in the world. From that day forward young Margaret lived with the fear of everything blowing up in her face, because she knew if education was what it would take to prepare her for the future, she wouldn't be prepared.

She knew very early in her childhood that she didn't like any-thing as structured and confining as school. At that young age, she didn't realize she had to go to school and apply herself to her studies in order to avoid the disaster her mother warned her happened to uneducated people.

Margaret knew instinctively that there was something lacking in her that was necessary for a person to be happy, and she could never figure out what that something was. Her mother had no idea what her prediction about her future did to Margaret that day and that it would damage her in ways she couldn't imagine, or that her daughter would remember it for the remainder of her life.

It was a lesson well learned, and Margaret never forgot it for a second however, I wonder if it was a lesson learned, or if it was some-thing more in the mind of the young child. All of her life she expected her mother's prediction to comes true, and it did however; not in the way, her mother thought it would happen.

Maybelle Mitchell was obsessed with her daughter getting an education thinking it would give her the advantage she would need to succeed in life without having to depend on a man for her livelihood. However; education was not a priority at the top of young Margaret's to do list. Frankly, I don't think education was what she needed as much as a stable happy home life, where she was confident that her parents loved her. If she could have had, confidence in what her future would be like, and her own abilities, without feeling the pressure for a formal education it might have made a difference in the way she turned out.

She was a person that fought everything she thought was being forced on her, all of her life, and the very thing she fought with everything she had, is what invaded her life in such a subtle way she didn't recognize it, and that was what ultimately destroyed her.

As a young girl she refused to conform to school rules, and requirements, and after her failure at college, she gave up on any educational endeavors, making her vulnerable to someone like John Marsh whose only interest in her was to write the book that had been his lifelong dream.

Margaret saw life with a different perspective than her mother did, although she wanted everything her mother wanted for her, she lacked the ambition, and self-discipline needed to achieve anything more than to read books, and write short stories that were never good enough for a publisher to accept. That was where she was when she met John Marsh. She had submitted short stories to publishers only to get them rejected.

She needed to be the center of attention in every situation, and she gravitated toward people who would give her that attention. The friends she made after she returned to Atlanta from Smith College were not acceptable to her family. They were as wild, and out of control as she was. Her home life was miserable; she felt her family would never accept anything she did.

She was so completely different from the other members of her family that she could not believe they would or could love her, especially her father who was very critical of her behavior. He never seemed to have time for her between his work, and other more important projects, with which he always seemed to be involved.

He never took the time to make her feel she was important as a human being, or that regardless of her chosen lifestyle, he accepted her as she was, and that he loved her. I don't think she felt loved by any of her family however; she was closer to her brother than any of the others after her mother died.

As a young child, she was so unhappy with her life that she fantasized about living in the past, a past that involved war and destruction that she was familiar with from listening to stories from her elder relatives who had lived through it, and had lost almost everything.

She made up stories and plays from her memory of the recollections of her older family members who were survivors of the civil war where she was sometimes the hero, and sometimes the heroine. At this stage of her life, she was confused about her identity, not sure, if she wanted to be a girl or a boy.

When she turned ten her mother replaced her boy pants with skirts, and sent her to dance class however; those efforts by her mother didn't erase her boyish walk, and tomboy personality, she couldn't change the damage that had already been done.

Her mother never exhibited feminine traits that most little girls emulate from their mother. Maybelle Mitchell was a women's rights activist that was always preaching her views with the force and manner of a strong willed man. She didn't set a feminine example for her daughter.

It was actually a personality trait instilled in her child's memory at the most critical time of her life when children are learning who they are.

She sensed her mother didn't like men, and she wasn't the traditional motherly type, and that was confusing to the young child, she couldn't understand why her parents were so different from those of her friends.

She loved the excitement of baseball, and the neighborhood baseball team accepted her as a pitcher, a position she kept until she was fourteen years old. During her lifetime she assumed two other names the tomboy "Jimmy" was one, and "Peggy the flamboyant flapper" was the other, this was the beginning of her "identity crisis" and multiple personalities.

When her mother was present and anyone asked her what she wanted to be when she grew up she always answered with whatever she thought her mother would approve of even though she knew at an early age that if education was a requirement she wasn't interested.

She grew up thinking because of the social status of her family that she didn't have to follow the rules in life that everyone else has to follow, she thought she could do whatever she wanted to do, that rules were for everyone else, and didn't apply to her. She didn't realize that there would come a time that she would be accountable for her own actions, and her family wouldn't be able to help her.

When her mother told her at the age of six how important education was, she made up her mind right then, that her mother could make her go to school, but no one could make her learn anything she didn't want to learn.

That was her attitude toward education that caused her as an adult to be incapable of making her own way, causing her to have to depend on John Marsh for her livelihood.

From a very young age she didn't think she needed to go to school to learn what she wanted to know. However, if she had been serious about being a doctor, or as she later said a psychiatrist, she would have known how important getting an education would have been to her.

Her mother wasn't pleased with her daughter's casual attitude toward the Catholic Church. At the age of ten, she was questioning her religious beliefs as well as her sexuality. She acted more like a boy than she did a girl, and she had become secretive about everything.

When she was eleven her mother's concern toward her daughter's secretive nature escalated. She never offered information about anything she was doing or planning to do. She was becoming independent, and didn't like anyone questioning anything she did.

If her mother had been listening to her daughter at this time in her life, her behavior would have raised a red flag that something unusual was happening to her. When she completed elementary school she had not excelled in anything therefore, she didn't receive any special recognition.

Then she went unwillingly to the Washington Seminary a private school for girls where she was required to act like a girl, follow rules, and act in accordance with socially accepted protocol that was like rubbing salt into a raw wound for her. This was where the women who would have a tremendous impact on her future would become aware of her unacceptable behavior.

She spent most of her time writing stories, and plays where she was living in a fantasy world. Those plays were a neighborhood affair, with the neighborhood children the actors. Some of the plays she wrote called for a boy to kiss a girl, when the neighborhood boys refused, she would then play the boy herself, and kiss the girl.

She didn't have a problem with it, because her personality was more male than it was female during that stage of her development, another instance of the "search for her identity".

Her life became so unpleasant that she pretended it didn't exist. Going to school was so distasteful to her that the only way she could deal with it was to fantasize about a happy exciting life that she had never before or ever would experience.

She went through the rest of her life without finding that elusive happiness everyone looks for, and some never find. That was what made her vulnerable to John Marsh, and his passion to write the great American novel, and his insistence that with her help they could do it.

It was written that her brother said the Washington Seminary didn't prepare his sister for college, and that she had been blackballed there without saying that the reason for that could have been her lack of interest in academics, and her rebellion against traditional dress, and inappropriate public conduct.

By this time in her life, she knew there was something seriously wrong with her that she was different from her friends. When Margaret, and her mother were deciding on a college for her to attend they decided on Smith College in North Hampton Massachusetts.

She spent nine months thinking if she could become a psychiatrist she could diagnose herself, and find out what was wrong with her. She didn't take into consideration the time, and effort it takes to be a doctor of any kind, if she had she would never have gone there.

Until she actually went to college, she didn't realize that to become a doctor it would take years of hard work and study. She wasn't willing to sacrifice her time or energy to become a doctor or anything else, she was enjoying her college days learning a bohemian lifestyle that was detrimental to her future, instead of concentrating on her studies that would have made her family proud of her.

MORALS OF AN
ALLEY CAT

A fter her mother died from the flu epidemic in 1919, she
returned home to Atlanta to "keep house" for her father
Eugene Mitchell, and her brother Stephens. Keeping
house for her meant telling the servants what to do, and keeping
them in line.

When she arrived in Atlanta, she learned that her maternal grandmother had moved into the Mitchell home to act as her chaperone,
making adjusting to being home again after her few months away at
college very difficult for her.

She had assumed a new name and a wild bohemian lifestyle that
she knew her father and grandmother would never accept in the

home, especially her grandmother who had strict ideas about the morals, and behavior of a young girl.

With a new personality, and her insistence that everyone call her "Peggy" the clash with her grandmother was swift, and unrelenting. Without her mother there to act as mediator between her father, and grandmother whose strict criticism of her left nothing for the imagination, she knew her home life with them would be a nightmare, because they didn't approve of anything she did.

Her Father and grandmother whose moral values were uncompromising clashed with the bohemian lifestyle Margaret flaunted in their face after she returned home from college.

The few months she was away at college she became more rebellious than she had ever been, and her behavior was unacceptable to both of them however, they didn't know how to handle her outbursts when she deliberately refused to comply with their rules.

The behavior she exhibited had not been caused by the college itself, however, she was exposed to influences possibly from friends she met while she was there, that she was not mature enough to handle, that swayed her thinking, and led her to embrace a lifestyle unacceptable to normal southern society.

She had never been educationally motivated, barely making passing grades through elementary, and high school. When her mother enrolled her in college, she was very immature, and should have waited until she was older to attend college.

Her prior experiences, along with whatever it was that she encountered there, had a devastating effect on her for the rest of her life. I think what happened to her in college related to what she later wrote to her friend Alan Edee about and that was her unusual sexual experiences.

Margaret knew there was something seriously wrong with her. However, she didn't want to admit what it was. She discussed sex and pornography with her friends, and she knew her problem stemmed somehow from unnatural sexual desire, that is different from a customary, traditional or generally accepted standard.

Margaret Mitchell knew she had mental problems from a very early age, and I wonder if Stephens advised her not to seek help for it the same way he advised John Marsh not to accept the Veterans benefit he was eligible for because of the stigma of mental illness that could surface years later and cause him social problems.

From the time she was three years old until she was fourteen everyone in her neighborhood called her "Jimmy" now she was "Peggy" this was her second personality, and it was about the bohemian lifestyle with no moral or sexual restraints.

She resented any outside intrusion into who she was or what she did. She acted with the morals of an "alley cat" she was bringing men into her fathers home late at night and they would stay until daylight allegedly "talking" causing her family to become more critical of her actions.

After her return from Smith College for winter season 1920/1921, she launched her career as a socialite by entering the Debutante Club that through her contempt for rules and protocol brought disgrace and anger to the Mitchell family when the Junior League refused to invite her to join their club.

The society women who were in charge of the Debutante Club were also in charge of the Junior League the most prestigious club in Atlanta, as well as the Washington Seminary. Those women were aware of Margaret and her rebellious nature from the private school she attended as a teenager therefore, they didn't need any introduction to her later.

"Peggy" who appeared after her return from Smith College was exhibiting behavior unacceptable to Atlanta Society or anyone with traditional values in that era. This behavior is what later led her, and a male friend to perform the L'Apache Dance that was so sensual, violent, and bizarre that it got her blackballed by Atlanta society.

She started hanging out at the March Hare Tea Shop on Auburn Avenue in a shabby part of Atlanta that was just a block from Peachtree Street better known to her, and her friends as "The Rabbit Hole". Where rebellious artistic, and lower social class people hung out.

She was drinking corn liquor, smoking cigarettes, using profanity, staying out late at night, hanging out in questionable establishments, and anything else she could think of to antagonize her father, and grandmother.

The purpose for belonging to the Debutante Club in the first place was for young women like her who had reached the age of maturity to present herself to "eligible bachelors" from her social class to find a husband.

That was what her family hoped would happen, but because of her reputation of being a party girl and her unbecoming public behavior that was never to be.

Margaret was a small pretty girl however; she had chosen a lifestyle that was definitely not acceptable to the matrons of Atlanta Society whose son's were those young bachelor's who were looking for wives.

Unfortunately for her family, the only men she was attracted to and who were attracted to her, were the wild ruthless type men like her first husband Red Berrien Upshaw whose lifestyle was also unacceptable to Traditional Atlanta Society.

By the time, she met Upshaw she already knew that men in her social class who were ready for marriage were not interested in her. Her attitude toward life at that time was to live the unconventional flapper lifestyle, where being promiscuous was acceptable, and tradition meant nothing to her, or to her friends.

She thought that because she was Margaret Mitchell that Atlanta Society would grant her approval without her having to conform to their rules. However, because they judged her by her own unacceptable public behavior and not by the reputation of her family, she spent the remainder of her life trying to get revenge.

Her father and brother had no idea what the future would hold for Margaret in Atlanta Society after the spectacle she made of herself at the charity dance where she and her partner performed the L'Apache Dance that was not only scandalous to the members of the Junior League it was a sensual extremely violent dance.

The Apache pronounced A-Posh or A-Poe-Shay Dance originated in the Parisian lower classes. In the U.S. it is pronounced like the Indian Tribe Apache however, there is no connection to the American Indian whatsoever.

The dance was performed in Paris in the Underworld Clubs. It was advertised as a dance of the underworld for valid reasons. Some of the women who danced the Apache died during their performance of broken back, neck etc. Margaret Mitchell could never have gotten approval from the members of the Junior League to perform such a violent dance if they had understood what it was.

The dance portrayed extreme male to female violence that according to my research, and one of her biographer's she experimented with violent sexual deviance going far beyond what was acceptable for young women in that era.

Some people thought that if the dance had been all she did, they might have overlooked the scandalous sensual violence of the dance; however, I doubt it would have been acceptable to Atlanta Society, or any person, or organization with traditional values at that time in history.

To add to her problems, she challenged the Junior League Members on where the money made from the charity ball was to go.

When put to the vote the members won, and afterward they refused to invite her to join their club.

Margaret and her father never forgave them for their rejection of her, and she spent the rest of her life seeking revenge because Atlanta Society had snubbed her. The L'Apache Dance performance was her way to flaunt her sexual preferences in the face of the club not realizing the backlash she would receive from it.

Margaret wrote Letters to her friend Allen Edee who was a student at Amherst located near Smith College where Margaret was a student for nine months, letter's describing her love life and how miserably unhappy she was after she returned home after her short stay at college.

Their friendship allowed them to become pen pals, and the letters she wrote to him explains how unstable, unhappy, and confused about her life, and her sexuality she really was.

When she wrote to him about trying to figure out what was missing in her life. She asked him if he knew what was wrong with her, that she knew there was something wrong because she was different from most of her friends however, she couldn't figure out what it was, she begged him if he knew to please tell her.

She told him she "couldn't love" that she would flirt, and tease men until they would "go crazy and force her" she said that was the only way she would have sex with them. In other words, "she would force them to rape her" to rationalize it she convinced herself that if she was "forced" it relieved her of any responsibility for the act.

On one occasion, she told him she was letting "five men" court her at the same time. She seemed obsessed with "men" and "sex", and for some reason she found it easy to write to him about her sex life perhaps because she knew he was knowledgeable on the subject, and his bohemian philosophy captivated her.

Years later, she told friends that the years from 1919 to 1921 were the unhappiest of her life. Those were the years she was baring her soul to Allen Edee while she was living in the Mitchell home under the watchful eye of her grandmother before John Marsh came into her life.

One night in 1920, Margaret, and her seventy-five year old grand-mother had such a violent altercation that her grandmother called a taxi-cab and moved all of her belongings out of the Mitchell home into the Georgian Terrace Hotel even though it was almost midnight.

In the 1920s, Atlanta was small enough that secrets were hard to keep, and the wild escapades Margaret Mitchell participated in were certainly not a secret to Atlanta Society.

What actually happened that night no one outside the family knows. Outsiders can only look at the situation they know about, and consider the possibilities. It definitely was not just a petty argument; it had to be much more than that to provoke her grandmother, and the Stephens family to turn on her.

Margaret and her grandmother clashed often over her behavior however, what her grandmother saw that night was different it was so shocking it caused an elderly woman to move out of her son-in-laws home in the middle of the night into a hotel.

Margaret always had a liking for corn liquor, and would brag about how well she could handle it when she would be out with her friends she felt it was her duty to see that they got home safely after a night of drinking and partying.

She would be the one to drive them home even though she had also been drinking; she thought nothing of driving under the influence of alcohol because "she could handle it". She thought the "law" didn't apply to her.

Her obsession with pornography may explain what was going on in the Mitchell home late at night after she returned home from Smith College that caused her grandmother to leave the home, and alienated the Stephens family from the Atlanta Mitchell's.

Biographer Darden Asbury Pyron the author of Southern Daughter portrayed Margaret as an avid collector of pornography. He said it was something that wasn't a secret among her friends, everyone who knew her knew about her "unusual sexual nature".

Pyron said people who knew her said she was particularly fond of the case studies of Havelock Ellis that she ordered from New York dirty bookstores. He said her favorite Ellis history involved a case of "male lust" so extreme as to enforce disregard for its object's sex or species.

Pyron put it rather briefly, and to the point, "she dreamed of satyr's" she loved Cabell, and she discovered other objects to satisfy her interest in "erotica". He said that From Cabell she branched out into other high cultural pornography.

She owned more of Havelock Ellis books than any other except Cabell. I wonder if her collection of pornographic material was included in the items her husband burned after her death.

Margaret found a very explicit advertisement from an expensive set of books that she was so fasinated with she framed it and hung it over their bed. She said most everyone who saw it was shocked, but couldn't take their eyes off of it.

If he didn't destroy the pornographic material she owned when he destroyed all of her other belongings including her clothes, and her important papers, what could have happened to it when he died? I haven't seen anything that said it is hanging on display in the Margaret Mitchell House.

JOHN MARSH

For her to live in such close quarters with John Marsh he had to know about her sexual deviance although I couldn't find anything to connect him to her sexual escapades, except for the parties they had over the years where they read pornography, and graphically discussed it.

Although it was a known fact that for years she continued to receive unexplained physical injuries, that sometimes took many months and sometimes years to heal. Injuries that were the kind atheletes, not housewives get.

After her marriage while John was at work she had, friends including men she had dated that he was aware of coming to the apartment while he was at work. This is another red flag that should have told people Margaret and John didn't have a traditional marriage

She commented to his sister how John was never jealous of her. That he let her continue to have all of the "beaus" she wanted in her life. What kind of man wouldn't be jealous of his new bride having her former men friends visiting her while he was at work.

My answer to that is he wasn't in love with her, He didn't stop that unusual behavior until he was ready for her to start the book. It was at that time that he cut her off from all of her friend's male and female.

She made it obvious that her relationship with him was nothing more than an "arrangement" or in her words "a bargain" to live together, and write a book, then in 1926, at his insistence she began to write the book that he had dreamed of writing his entire adult life.

John had the education, and the determination to write the Great American Novel, he just didn't have the material, the imagination or the talent to take ordinary things, and people and embelish until they were believable.

He was always on the lookout for someone he could recruit to help him with his goal to be a famous writer, and luckily he finally found it, and he had no intention of letting her get away from him regardless of what he had to do to inlist her help.

Margaret had everything he lacked except the education, and literary experience along with the fact that she became bored, and lost interest quickly, which was a problem for John.

John was five years older than Margaret, he was born October 6. 1895 in Maysville Kentucky his father died when he was ten years old causing his mother to have to go outside the home to find a job to support her five children.

John was the only one of the Marsh children who had physical challenges that kept him from joining his brothers and sisters in outdoor games and other childhood activities.

He stayed on the sidelines and watched their interactions with each other, to learn the things that didn't come to him naturally, as they do to normal children. I believe this was the beginning of his psychopathy.

He also developed an early reputation for emotional indifference, and independence that followed him throughout his life that caused some people to refer to him as "that slug".

John had scarlet fever in his early childhood, a disease that was contagious and required him to be quarantined from his brothers and sisters for a considerable amount of time.

This illness and the separation occurring during his formative years could have had a mental effect on him that caused him to become psychopathic, and suffer with the psychosomatic disorder he was diagnosed with for the remainder of his life.

It could have weakened his heart, and contributed along with his heavy smoking habit to the heart problems he suffered from later in his life. However, it didn't keep him out of the military, and he showed no evidence of having a heart problem for many years after leaving military service.

He was the only one of the Marsh children that took an interest in his father's newspaper business, and he was the only one of them to follow in his fathers footsteps to become a newspaperman. He was never successful as a reporter, but he excelled as an editor.

John had other ambitions as well, he had a lifelong desire to become a famous writer a man of literature however; he was fully aware that he didn't have the artistic ability needed to become one. In order to achieve that goal he would also need a marketable subject that he didn't have at that time, although he was always alert to the possibility that he would find one.

When he met Margaret Mitchell he was "ecstatic" he knew immediately he had hit the Jackpot, she had everything he was looking for and more. After he met her and realized her talent was what he needed he had no intention of ever letting her get away from him.

After leaving the military in 1919, he returned to his hometown of Maysville Kentucky. After a short visit with his family, he went back to Lexington to the newspaper where he had worked prior to going into the military.

After a few months he decided not to stay in Lexington, he moved on to Atlanta where there were more opportunities to find what he was looking for. He got a job as a reporter at the Daily Georgian Newspaper.

Then he moved into a boarding house just a block from the Georgian Terrace Hotel on West Peachtree Street putting him in the neighborhood where he would later meet Margaret Mitchell who had recently returned to Atlanta from Smith College.

He already had everything he needed except the artistic talent needed to write stories with "flair and embellish until it was impressive and magnificent".

That was what he was looking for in everyone he met, and he knew his opportunity to become that famous writer he wanted to be was more likely to happen in Atlanta than it was in Kentucky.

John was twenty-six years old when he met Margaret Mitchell. He was well educated, and intelligent however; he had no interest in having a permanent relationship with any woman, especially one with her personality, and background that he knew his conservative family would have a problem accepting although his mother didn't interfere into the lives of her children he knew she would have an opinion whether she said anything to him about it or not.

He just needed to find access to a marketable subject to write about. Therefore, his attraction to the artistic community and to artistic people was necessary, if he were ever going to meet someone who could help him achieve his dream.

When he met Margaret Mitchell, he had a job as a newspaper man who worked long hours, he was looking forward to a successful future in the newspaper business, along with his literary dream of becoming a famous writer someday.

He steadily moved toward writers, and other "creative charismatic" people such as those who hung out in unusual places such as the March Hare Tea Room better known to Margaret Mitchell and her friends as the "Rabbit Hole" where people whose personalities stood out in contrast to his own dull unemotional persona, whose level of energy evoked slur's such as "that slug" to describe him.

He was always impressed with people who had a much stronger outward personality than he had. People like Margaret Mitchell, and Red Upshaw. He attached himself to Margaret because of her story telling talent, and her southern background.

He befriended Red Upshaw because he was flamboyant and completely different from himself. Everything I could find about Red Upshaw said John didn't meet him for some time after he met Margaret.

The first time John saw Margaret was at the March Hare Tearoom the "Rabbit Hole" sitting on a table with her legs dangling telling stories, as he watched, and listened to her, he realized she was a talented storyteller, with the ability to dramatize, and embellish even the simplest story into something grand and after listening to her for several minutes he knew, she had what he was looking for.

Although he realized she needed some cleaning up, her grammar was horrible, and she used a lot of unnecessary profanity and sexual content. He knew he could overcome those flaws, it would just take some time.

It was obvious she lacked in formal education however, she had everything else he needed, she had the artistic talent background and southern material to write a novel about the Civil War, and the battle of Atlanta, and he had the education and journalistic ability she would need to write it.

John Marsh the intelligent educated man he was knew he had stumbled upon a "gold mine" all wrapped up in a small pretty girl. What he didn't know was how long it would take, and the extent of the trouble he would have to go through to remove all of the obstacles that would stand in the way of his "total domination" of her life.

At that time he had never even talked to her, nor had he figured out a "strategy "that he thought would work to convince her that his help was what she would need. All of that would have to come later. Before she became aware of his presence, he stood in the background watching and listening analyzing her as he did as a child when he learned by watching and listening to other children to learn how they interacted with each other and how they expressed their emotions.

John Marsh was not one to make his feelings or intentions known to anyone especially someone he had just met in a public place. He didn't put much stock in the opinion of others however, he did ask another person there who she was, he didn't think she would be interested in someone like him. However, that didn't deter him from making it his business to meet her.

Little did they know what fate had in store for them. He didn't know he was about to meet the most "morally unrestrained" and "daring person" he would ever know and she didn't know she was about to meet the man who would "dominate" and "control" every aspect of her life for twenty-four years someone who in the end would throw her under a moving car and kill her.

Shortly thereafter he was spending a great deal of time with her talking and learning everything there was to know about her. He was fascinated at her knowledge of the Civil War and old Atlanta.

He immediately started injecting himself as an invaluable partner in her life in such a way, that she was never able to overcome the influence he had over her. She didn't know it but her life was no longer her own, she was not aware of just how much control he planned to eventually have over her.

He knew what he would have to do to get her cooperation would have to be subtle underhanded. and deceptive enough to hide his true intentions.

He didn't want her to know what he had in mind for her was a plan that would take away everything that made Margaret Mitchell the flamboyant in your face, in charge everyone look at me person that she was.

He was aware that he didn't have the sex appeal or good looks of some of the local men in her social class. He was not financially secure therefore; the only thing he had to offer her was his journalistic ability, education and the promise that if she would do what he told her to do he would make her rich, and famous. Although at that time, she didn't really believe she could ever become a published author.

He would learn later that he had something else that she would be more interested in sharing with him than becoming a writer and that was freedom from her hated home life.

He was an outsider without the financial means to give her more than the bare necessities he was not in her social class he was five years older than she was and acted much older than he actually was.

They were completely different as far as personality. I suspect that after the disgraceful display she made of herself at the Junior League charity ball her family realized she would never get anyone in their social class to marry her, and they were probably grateful that anyone would consider her for a wife.

Margaret was attracted to men who were very different from John. In spite of her fathers objections she was attracted to men who were good looking who had the same wild, arrogant, unconventional attitude that she had.

What attracted her to John and separated him from other men was certainly not his looks, because he was not a good looking man he had absolutely no sex appeal however; he presented himself to her in a way that she trusted him, and found him very easy to talk with about anything that came to her mind. He had very quickly gained her trust, and took full advantage of it.

She was well aware that the men in her social class were not interested in her and that she didn't stand a chance of landing a husband who knew her reputation in Atlanta.

She didn't know what she was going to do to escape her father's home where he made her life miserable, and where her grandmothers close scrutiny of her unacceptable behavior drove her mad.

With John's use of language and his vocabulary, she knew right away that he was intelligent well educated and independent. What she wanted more than anything in the world was independence from her family, and she wanted to become a published writer, although she was aware that she had neither the education, nor the discipline to achieve that goal she also knew he had what she lacked.

Soon after they met she learned he shared her desire to be a writer although he actually had the education and journalistic ability needed to be a published author he didn't possess the artistic talent nor did he have a marketable subject to write about.

He soon learned she had both of those crucial elements that he would need. She knew instinctively that he could be an asset to her writing ambitions and the possibility was there that he could help her escape from her father's home as well.

He wanted to know all there was to know about this unusual person who was obviously uneducated, with low self esteem who didn't have a clue what to do with her talent however; he knew what to do with it, and from that day forward he was obsessed with her southern background that he knew he could use to his advantage.

She was immediately willing to tell him all about herself and her background everything she told him was fascinating to him letting him know his evaluation of her was on target. He knew what she had was what he needed and he would do whatever he had to do for as long as it would take to convince her that he could make them rich and famous.

It is important to understand why John was so determined to use what he knew most likely would never come along again in his lifetime to his advantage. He knew he had to be careful not to let her know what he had in mind.

What he was about to embark on was not going to be easy, and if she found out what he was really after it could be over as quickly as it had started.

She had never excelled at anything she had a reputation of being a party girl and a party girl was the last thing John Marsh wanted in his life however; he saw her potential and he listened to her trying unsuccessfully at first to convince her that together they could become rich and famous which was impossible for either of them to do alone.

However, he had a long way to go to convince her of the value of his plans for them. I don't think he was ever successful in building her confidence in her own writing skills because she was never successful in getting anything she had written on her own published causing her to doubt her writing abilities.

It never occurred to her that everything she had always thought of as unimportant about education and learning she would now need if she were to become a successful writer.

In those days they didn't have access to a word processor or internet therefore, they had to do everything the hard way, and that along with John working a full time job, is why it took him so long to edit and re-write "Gone with the Wind".

John Marsh graduated from the University of Kentucky with a Bachelor of Arts Degree, with a major in English. He also took three courses in journalism excelling in everything making him the perfect writing partner for Margaret who didn't have any educational background that would provide her the ability to be a writer or to be successful at anything.

Her only contribution would have to be her knowledge of the Civil War, old Atlanta, and her love of the south. The young Margaret having a vivid imagination and memory could visualize the stories she read, and listened to from her older family members, as she sat on their laps, listening to their stories full of profanity she was memorizing every word, learning how to curse picturing in her mind the scenes they were describing as if she were living it.

Early in their relationship, when John suggested reading material to her she quickly told him she didn't like anyone telling her what to read. At that time he had not gained complete control over everything she did. It would take her marrying Red Upshaw and two years of that publicly humiliating failure to break her down enough for him to take over her life as he eventually did.

He knew without a doubt if she ever got the idea that he was trying to control her he would be finished. He had to take his time patience was the key.

Although he was always methodical and manipulative, he couldn't let her know what he had in mind for her. Fearing she would recognize what he was planning he had to move slowly and agree with what he considered her bizarre behavior although it was not an easy thing for him to do.

After dating him steadily for a while she became more sensitive about his passion for literature and agreed to read some of the books he suggested although it took years she eventually began to enjoy it more. She never completely fell in love with it however; at his insistence she sometimes read what he chose for her with a bad taste in her mouth. She still preferred to make her own choice about what she read.

Her lifestyle made John cringe, at those times he would take a deep breath and continue never veering off track. He took one obstacle at a time to deal with the first being her whirlwind social life nearly all of her friends were getting married, her days, and nights were filled with social events that kept her busy.

Her life was not like the lives of the women in his family her lifestyle was not one he could live with and he had no intention of ever accepting it. He thought he could change her if given enough time. The only thing on his mind was what they could do to advance the book that had become his obsession.

He didn't complain however, he just worked in a determined methodical way until he cut her off from her friends, and completely changed everything about her former life.

Margaret felt shame for her failure to complete her education she was fearful about her future. John had his work cut out for him if he was going to convince her she could do any of the things he had planned for her it meant he would have to provide the education she didn't receive when she was younger.

Without alerting her to his desire he had to change everything about her to something more in line with the lives of the women in his family that he could accept and live with. He knew it would be a monumental task that he wasn't sure he could pull off.

Shortly after they met they were spending a great deal of time together up until that time her life had been constantly busy, and hurried with lack of time to rest or relax creating an atmosphere of things barely under control. John saw her lifestyle as something he could never accept therefore; he would do everything in his power to change it.

Margaret once described herself as a firebrand type of woman. Which is a strong aggressive personality that encourages unrest she was the complete opposite of him and was not the kind of woman that one would expect John Marsh to become involved with, especially to live with for twenty-four years without some kind of negative reaction.

Both Margaret and John had illnesses that were both physical and mental that influenced their lives. After he became her confidant and learned how vulnerable she would be to someone like him they talked about everything this was the beginning of his effort to make her believe she couldn't live without him.

With the mental illness that both of them suffered, John's being the most serious, and bizarre their relationship had to come to a conclusion eventually. I've asked myself a million times since I started reading about the kind of man John was, and the kind of relationship they had if there could have been any other ending except a violent one.

UPSHAW MARRIAGE

J ust when John thought he had her convinced that he was the man for her Red Berrien Upshaw came on the scene and John soon found out that his relationship with her was not on solid ground.

What attracted her to Upshaw John knew he didn't have and that any relationship he might ever have with her would have to be platonic based the fact that he never wanted a close sexual relationship with a woman.

She started dating both of them at the same time. She would go out with one of them, then when she returned from that date the other one would be waiting for her then they would go on their date this went on until she finally told John she was going to marry Red Upshaw. Margaret and everyone who knew them were very surprised at his reaction.

When she told her family, and friends she was going to marry Red Upshaw they were shocked although not as much as they were at John's reaction to the marriage that was not how someone would have reacted if he had been in love with her.

He was not in love with her then or ever, he was there as a friend of both the bride and groom to help in any way he could to make sure the marriage took place on schedule. It was something John wanted to happen. He knew the sooner they were married the sooner she would be available to help him with his future plans for her.

She married Red Upshaw in September 1922, and her divorce became final on October 16, 1924, she was married to him for two years, but the marriage was off and on.

He would show up after being away for long periods of time that she didn't know where he was then unexpectedly he would show up again and they would get back together for a short time then he would disappear again.

She accused him of beating her one last time, before she finally went through with the divorce at the urging of her father brother and John. When the marriage to Upshaw failed as John had predicted it would and she was a divorced woman he moved in very quickly take-ing over control of her life.

After her divorce from Upshaw she knew she needed to start a new life to do that she would have to have a way to make herself a liv-ing. She didn't want to be dependent on her father for all of her needs that made her feel obligated to follow his rules when he was her sole means of support.

Red Upshaw was not the kind of man her family wanted her to marry they never took into consideration that she was in love with him as much as she was capable of being in love with a man. She had made the statement to her friend that "she couldn't love" and her history tells a story of it's own. If she was ever in love it wasn't something she recognized.

Her relationship with Upshaw ended the same way Scarlett's relationship ended with Rhett. She didn't know until he left her that she was in love with him. I think what she thought was love was the need to belong.

Margaret didn't know she was in love with Red Upshaw until the marriage was over and that was because she knew he was gone and would never return for good, it was always just a temporary relationship for them.

When he left and she knew he would never return to have a life with her was the reason why she refused to give the book a happy ending. She had never experienced happiness in a relationship therefore; she couldn't bring herself to write about something she had never experienced.

She talked about her first husband Red Upshaw who was always on her mind, for the rest of her life to Medora Perkerson who was the wife of the editor of the Atlanta Journal and a personal friend of hers.

Red Upshaw confronted Margaret on several occasions, and asked her if she was still in love with him that he thought she was. She asked him why he thought that, and he answered because of what she had written in her book that he thought she had based Rhett Butler, and Scarlett on their life together.

After that is when she became fearful of what he might do. She wasn't afraid he would physically abuse her she was afraid he would challenge her on her the characters in the book. He knew the book described the relationship they shared, and what she wrote about was what happened between them.

The only thing John could have done to stop her from marrying Upshaw was to propose to her himself, and judging from his reaction to marriage when it was finally his turn to marry her he could not have proposed to her or married her under any circumstances.

At that time his obsession with the book he knew they could write together had not risen to the extent that he would do anything even marry her to further his agenda. however; it did eventually become that important to him.

What he wanted from Margaret was not sex, or marriage, and he knew if she married Upshaw it would be a temporary situation, because neither of them had enough self-discipline, or responsibility to make a marriage work for very long, and after it ended she would be easily manipulated.

She never thought about what John's motive for becoming a part of her life could be. She never considered that sex was not what he wanted from her, that he was a "wolf in sheep clothing" with an agenda that she could not even imagine.

To get what he wanted from her he had to wait until her world blew up in her face as her mother had predicted it would, and she was completely vulnerable. John knew he just had to stand back and wait, and that it wouldn't take long.

He would have preferred to move on with his plans for her, but he had miscalculated how long it would take for the divorce from Red Upshaw to become final. It never occurred to him that it would take two years. Especially after, she told him after only being married for a month that she wanted out of the marriage.

The injuries she said she sustained from Upshaw during the marriage could have been from "rough sex", and may be why for years prior to her death she expressed guilt that the divorce was her fault.

How could she explain to her father, and brother the black eye, and bruises when she came out of the bedroom she shared with Upshaw without telling them he beat her. I don't think for a minute that she would have told them that it was from rough sex.

After her divorce from Upshaw where she accused him of beating her as her grounds for divorce she continued to have unexplained broken bones, bruises and other injuries that she had no explanation for, that she could have sustained from rough sex, and Red Upshaw wasn't always around when those injuries occurred, many of them after her marriage to John Marsh.

The only feeling she had for John at that time was that he would take care of her, she felt safe with him. He had done everything he knew to do, and nothing had worked for him, he still was not where he wanted to be with her although he never failed to stay in constant contact with her, even though she was a married woman.

He knew a failed marriage, and divorce in those days was unacceptable to society, and especially to someone like her, with a Catholic background. Red Upshaw was John's roommate, and friend, he knew enough about Red, and his lifestyle to know the marriage would fail very quickly, and he would be there to pick her up, and help her get through it.

I think John orchestrated the marriage to Upshaw knowing it would fail, and it would open the door for him to take advantage of her. He knew that a divorce was what it would take to convince her that he was what she needed in her life.

He thought that after the marriage ended she would want a relationship that wouldn't require intimacy, that security, and to escape her hated life in her father's home would appeal to her more.

She had told John when they first met that she preferred to be called Peggy, her personality that was the wild side of her that recklessly married Red Upshaw, and frowned on everything her father and grandmother tried to tell her she was doing wrong.

John was particularly fond of her Peggy character that was the happy, anything goes, easy to manipulate side of her, unlike Margaret who was more direct, and to the point, who was not easily manipulated and controlled she was the one he learned to hate after being confined to the apartment with her for almost two years prior to her death.

Unfortunately one of the things that attracted Margaret to John was the fact that he never screamed and yelled when he was angry in the way her family did, nor did he seem to get excited about anything.

He didn't show emotion under extreme stress. When he got mad, he spoke in a calm even tone, never raising his voice, this could explain why their Maid Bessie Jordan and secretary Margaret Baugh never heard him when he was angry with her.

Margaret knew he didn't make idle threats that he meant everything he said those last years after the book was published, and they had nothing to talk about, they no longer had a common goal, and the "bargain" was no longer relevant.

Her own family was very emotional and outspoken when something was happening they didn't like and John's lack of emotion should have been a "red flag" that something was seriously wrong with him.

I think as time went by she did realize there was a lot more to John Marsh than she could have ever imagined. He was methodical and manipulative however; she didn't see that in him until much later, when it was too late to do anything about it.

When she learned he had been an English teacher she realized right away that he was capable of teaching her what she needed to know to become a writer, but she wasn't sure she was up to the task of learning what he wanted to teach her. She had never had patience with such things.

She had been writing short stories since she was a child, and had sent some of her work to publishers only to have it rejected. Rejection from publishers was very hard for Margaret it made her doubt her ability to be an author.

Although she had never been successful in getting anything she wrote published, she was aware that writing was something that didn't require much formal education, therefore she told everyone that a "writer" was what she wanted to be not realizing that she would still need more education than she had.

Soon after she met John she learned that his desire to be a famous writer was much greater than hers, and that he had the education, experience, and self-discipline to be successful. She knew that for her to ever succeed as a writer that she had to have his help; otherwise she didn't know what she would do with her life.

To understand John you have to know how he hid his true intention to dominate, and control her life, using subtle underhanded, deception. Margaret was a high strung, opinionated person. With a lot of pride, but little self esteem.

If she had ever suspected what John had in mind for her, that would have been the end of their relationship, she would have dropped him regardless of the consequences, destroying any chance of him ever acquiring her help to write a book.

When she met John she had never thought about how valuable her childhood stories on the laps of the old Civil War Veterans who told her stories about their military experience, and the battle of Atlanta would be to her in the future.

She had no idea that her Civil War, and old Atlanta stories were what attracted John Marsh to her in the first place, and what John saw in her was his chance to write the Great American Novel that had been his lifelong dream.

She remembered everything her family had told her about the battle's they had been in, and when she repeated some of it to John he knew right away what it would mean for the future.

He knew that with his help they could write a novel about the Civil War, that he could get published. Although she had never been able to get anything she had written accepted by a publisher, with his input she thought they might have a chance to write something that he could get published.

JOB ATLANTA JOURNAL

T he Atlanta Journal was the only public employment Margaret Mitchell ever had. After she filed for a divorce from Red Upshaw John talked her into applying for a job against the will of her father and brother at the newspaper where he was employed.

John was already working at the Atlanta Journal, and although she had never used a typewriter, or had a job or work experience of any kind John went to the editor of the newspaper, and without telling him she didn't have any experience he asked him to hire her.

John and Margaret lied to the editor of the Atlanta Journal to get her a job, just as John Marsh lied on the witness stand against my dad, and to the police before his trial.

When John asked his boss Angus Perkerson to hire Margaret without telling him she had never had a job, he told him to send her in to talk to him, but before she went in, they made up a work history, of what she would say in the interview

With no job experience or typing ability, she got the job by lying to the editor telling him she had worked at the Springfield Republican, when in fact she had never had a job, and had never used a typewriter in her life. Without conspiring with John Marsh to deceive the editor of the newspaper, she didn't have a chance of getting the job.

Margaret Mitchell worked at the Atlanta Journal for four years knowing she had told bald-faced lies to get the job. She knew Angus Perkerson, and his wife Medora were aware that John had made it possible for her to work there with no experience or typing ability by doing most of her work for her.

Angus Perkerson once made the statement that Peggy Mitchell wrote "like a man" the reason she wrote like a man was that a man "John Marsh re-wrote her articles before she turned them in to the newspaper just like he re-wrote "Gone With the Wind".

I don't think the Perkerson's were so uninformed that they didn't know, or at least suspect that John and Margaret had told lies to get her hired at the Journal. I suspect they did know, and chose not to confront them with it.

Margaret who had always wanted to be one of the boys fit perfectly into the men's world at the newspaper. There were not very many female reporters in the early 1920s, making her feel privileged that she could get such a job. However, the men employed there were in awe of a young girl whose cursing ability was equal to their own.

This was a world where she could feel free to use the profanity she had learned, and used since she was a small child sitting on the laps of her elder male relatives who had fought in the Civil War, and cursed profusely.

John got her the job where she would write the stories that was her strong point, and he made sure, before she turned her work in that he had edited, and corrected her spelling, punctuation, bad grammar, and removed the profanity, and sexual content or anything that would have been unacceptable to the editor for publication, just as he did later with "Gone with the Wind".

After John met Margaret, his family thought he had changed his mind about how he felt about women. He had never had many relationships with the opposite sex, and he considered himself old in his late twenties.

He made it no secret how he felt about women and marriage. He said he couldn't imagine not becoming bored with any woman after a certain length of time of close confinement.

His thoughts on women, and marriage that he related to his mother tells me he never wanted to marry anyone however; his desire to write a book, and become famous was far stronger than his distaste for women, and marriage.

After her divorce from Red Upshaw in 1924, and she had been working at the Atlanta Journal for about a year John realizing he had to act if he was going to have her southern knowledge to write the book that was his dream, he relented and asked her to marry him.

They talked about where they would live, and thinking her life would improve if she could just get out from under her fathers control, she agreed to marry him.

John had never made any sexual demands on her, and her attachment to him was not of a sexual nature, she didn't see him as a sensual or sexual person. She saw in him what he wanted her to see. She never suspected the kind of man he really was, and unfortunately, for her she trusted him.

She never questioned his past relationships, or lack thereof with women. His demeanor was calm, and she never saw him lose his temper the way her family so often did.

Her respect for his education and intelligence didn't let her see the man who was almost invisible to others; she saw in him what she wanted desperately to see. and by her lack of understanding his personal agenda allowed him to control and manipulate her for twenty-four years.

Bizarre Illness

They set a wedding date for Valentine Day February 14, 1925. As the wedding day came, closer and closer John began to feel panic. How was he going to be able to live in close confinement, married to a woman? It was something he had told his mother he could not do.

After he asked Margaret to marry him and she accepted a few days passed that he had time to think about what he was about to do. when he realized it was a done deal it was such a shock to his psyche that he had a complete physical breakdown.

A Breakdown that turned out to be one of the most bizarre psychosomatic health issues known to the health profession at that time. He started hiccupping, and hiccupped for thirty-one days until he almost died.

Margaret knew she would have to check him into the hospital because she wouldn't be able to work at the Journal, and nurse him at the same time. She checked him into the Saint Joseph Infirmary where he grew progressively worse.

His seizures destroyed their plans for the wedding. His condition continued to worsen every day until the doctors gave up hope that he would survive, and told her they needed to contact his family. She gave the hospital the information they needed to get in touch with them and his brother Henry arrived a few days later.

His condition continued to worsen until their planned wedding day passed. The following days his condition began to improve slowly he had escaped a situation that would have been disastrous to someone with his negative perception of marriage and the close confinement with a woman after marriage.

When his doctor told her the only possible explanation was psychosomatic, her response was disbelief. At first, she refused to believe his illness was all in his mind, and she made her opinion known to the doctor that she didn't believe that he was so appalled at marriage to her that his subconscious mind took over, and made him physically ill.

After his release from Saint Joseph Infirmary at the end of March 1925, after two month's in the hospital, Margaret took him to her fathers' home to recuperate. John never showed emotion therefore, the only outward evidence of a mental condition afterward was his frequent hospitalizations where the doctors couldn't find any medical reason for his condition, and his epileptic seizures became more frequent.

Afterward when anything happened that put a lot of stress on him it would trigger his psychosomatic illness that would manifest itself in many ways this illness may have been one of the secrets she admitted they shared.

In June 1925, thinking John's health issues were over, they began to plan for another wedding day. They were sitting in the parlor in the Mitchell home one day when John suddenly stopped talking in mid sentence, and became quiet.

She looked at him in horror as he had a seizure, she had never seen anything like that before, and it was a frightening experience for her.

Margaret thinking he was dying screamed for her father and brother when suddenly he was back to normal, and didn't realize anything had happened. She said he stared down at his burned hand where he had been holding a cigarette with a puzzled look on his face.

He suffered those seizures regularly for the rest of his life without warning, and when it happened in public, it was an embarrassment to them. When they were out in public, she watched him closely to make sure she would catch it if he had a seizure where she could make sure he didn't become a public spectacle.

She never wanted anything personal about her, or John to appear in a public forum before or after the book was published that would give anyone a close look at their personal life. They were very secretive, and in my opinion, no one is that secretive unless they have something to hide. Their lives after their marriage definitely was not what most people would consider normal.

On June 15, 1925, Margaret and John went to the Fulton County Courthouse in Atlanta to get their marriage license. On the evening of July 4, 1925, they were married at the Unitarian Universalist Church on West Peachtree Street in Atlanta Georgia.

John and Margaret stayed together for twenty-four years, they never had children, causing some people to think he was gay, or he lacked sexual drive, and that is not a surprise to me considering his admission that he smoked five packs of cigarettes a day.

A smoking habit that extensive certainly could make a man impotent, and cause all kinds of physical maladies such as heart disease, that we know he had. That heart condition was what he died from just two years after Margaret died.

John went to the Veterans Hospital for a general examination a few weeks after their honeymoon, and to his surprise, the doctor there reached the same diagnosis as the doctor's at Saint Joseph, that his series of bizarre illnesses were of a psychosomatic origin, and that he was qualified to receive a monthly compensation check from the Veterans Administration.

Because he would have had to sign a document that would conclude he had an emotional, or mental illness that could surface someday, and be an embarrassment, he declined the pension, after consulting with Stephens Mitchell who advised him against accepting it.

Marrying any woman would have been a huge issue for John, who never thought changing his habits to suit those of a woman would be worth the effort. However, to marry a woman with Margaret Mitchell's background would have been a very traumatic experience for him, one that could easily have triggered his psychosomatic illness.

A reasonable person would conclude that before they made wedding plans for the second time John Marsh would have insisted on an agreement that they would marry in name only to write the book. That would have allowed him to marry her without the fear that she would expect more than he was willing, or was physically able to give her.

When they made the bargain to get married both of them knew it would be a sacrifice. She would have to give up her active social lifestyle, he would have to give up his treasured privacy, and live in close quarters with a woman.

That was the last thing in the world he would have wanted to do under normal circumstances however; he had to either marry her or forget his dream of becoming the famous writer he had told his mother he hoped to be.

He would have to give up his freedom, and the things he enjoyed doing that he considered important for the time it would take to write the book.

At that time he had no idea how many years of hard work, and deprivation he would have to endure living with a woman who was inundated with illnesses, and injuries for which there was never any explanation.

It was a bargain made between Margaret whose desire was for someone to take care of her, and John's desire to write the Great American Novel, when suddenly they found themselves at an impasse, in an era when they couldn't live together unmarried. They had to find a solution that would allow them to live together where he could guide her in the direction he wanted her to go,

Then they came up with "the marriage that was actually nothing more than a business transaction" that John could accept, and live with on a daily basis.

It would allow him to have close contact with Margaret to make sure she stayed focused on the project that changed their relationship in his mind to a "business arrangement" that she referred to as a" bargain".

Unfortunately, for two people whose vision of marriage was unacceptable for many reasons they had to make a bargain that would allow them to live together without causing gossip. Margaret was no more interested in a romantic relationship with John than he was with her however; It was the only way they could live together to write the book that turned out to be "Gone with the Wind".

From the time of their marriage, their lives took on new meaning. They moved into his one bedroom apartment they named "the dump" that would have taken very little work to keep it clean, however; she looked at it as a job for servants and beneath her to do domestic work, she hated anything to do with cooking or housekeeping.

The first thing she did after the marriage was to make "name-plates" and hang them next to the front door of the apartment. The first one with "Margaret Mitchell", the other "John Marsh" where anyone coming to the door would know who lived there.. She soon had to change them to one nameplate with Mr. and Mrs. John Marsh in response to curiosity from visitors concerning their marital status.

Their relationship was not traditional therefore; they didn't act like a married couple. The nameplate with her maiden name on it then later her maiden name on the book suggested that she didn't ever consider herself married to John Marsh.

They had a problem adjusting to married life; it was something both of them had sworn an oath never to do. He never wanted a close relationship with any woman, and after her divorce from Red Upshaw, a platonic marriage for convenience was what she wanted. John being a neat person couldn't live in the clutter, and filth that didn't seem to bother her.

I couldn't find one instance where he confronted her about it, but of course as in all marriages, what goes on behind closed doors usually stays there.

Both of them were smokers, he said he smoked 60 cigarettes a day. Five packs of cigarettes a day is a huge health hazard that finally caught up with him. John Marsh was not a normal man, he was a man with a plan, determined to become a rich and famous writer regardless of the hardship he would have to endure. He had a personal motivation to reach his goal.

When you take a man who has absolutely no appeal to women, and someone like Margaret Mitchell for whom firebrand is a perfect description. Then put them together in a small one-bedroom apartment, with barely enough money to survive on, and gradually cut her off from her friends except for special occasions, and you have a "disaster" in the making.

He soon discovered when he would arrive home after a hard days work, the house was in a mess, and there was no meal started, that she didn't have any cooking or housekeeping skills, and even if she knew how to do any of those things, she would have refused to do them, because she thought it beneath her.

In her mind, those were jobs for servants. She had a strong dislike for housekeeping, no matter how messy the apartment got, or how many dirty ashtrays there was from both of them smoking, she never cleaned anything up.

In the beginning he tried to learn to cook, and do the cleaning himself. In addition to working long hours at his job, but finally growing weary of coming home to find the apartment in a mess, and having to shop for groceries, and cook their evening meal himself, he decided to figure out a way to hire a part time housekeeper and cook.

John knew Margaret despised doing domestic work, and he realized she was never going to keep house the way his mother, and the women in his family had always done, and there was no point in ever expecting her to emulate his family in any way.

He also knew those things were not the top issues on his agenda, and that to reach his goal he would have to accept that his wife did not want the same things out of life that he wanted, and get on with important things.

At first, he hired a part time cook and housekeeper, and a woman to do the laundry; this helped him out tremendously, although they needed someone full time.

It was at that time when Eugene Mitchell sent his housekeeper Bessie Jordan to keep house, and cook for them, and she worked for them the remainder of their lives. She stayed and worked for John after he moved into his new home after Margaret died, and continued to keep house for him until his death.

John's methodical personality and his flaw picking were not easy to live with as Margaret soon found out. It took special effort and tolerance on her part to accept his odd mannerisms, already set in his ways he didn't want surprises of any kind.

He hated unfamiliar food, uninvited company, and he detested overnight guests, the complete opposite of the lifestyle she preferred. Luckily, their apartment was so small that it was something they didn't have to deal with often.

Margaret married John to escape from her father's home where she felt restrained from living the bohemian lifestyle she had chosen for herself. She didn't realize she had traded the "witch" for a "devil". She didn't know he had an agenda that she had no clue he had, that would turn her life into what he wanted it to be.

What she soon found out after the marriage was that John Marsh was not the saintly, wonderful man he portrayed himself to be. His intentions toward her were never to help her; it was to use her southern experience, and story telling talent to help him fulfill his dream to write a book.

He knew if he had to conform to her less than pleasant lifestyle, and help out doing housework after working at his job all day he was willing to do it for as long as it took.

At first, I couldn't understand how she could move out of her father's mansion into a one-bedroom apartment with John Marsh, and live in poverty for years by choice until I read about her home life with her father and grandmother who were openly opposed to her lifestyle.

She knew as long as she lived in his home she would have to abide by his rules, and she would have done anything to escape from her father and his control over her.

She thought because John was not jealous of her that she could continue her unconventional lifestyle. What she didn't realize was that her decision to marry him would change her lifestyle in ways she couldn't even imagine.

It took him a year, but he finally had her cut off from her friends, and confined to a small one-bedroom apartment where they lived until 1932 when John got a promotion, and a raise allowing them to move to a much larger nicer apartment.

WRITING GONE WITH THE WIND

I n reading about them, and studying every step of their evolvement from the time they met, until they died, is an extraordinary story to say the least. I was fascinated by the way, he manipulated and controlled her every action making sure she read the right books on the subject he wanted for the book.

On his way from work the first year after their marriage, John would go by the library, and bring home arms full of books for her to read. Books that he knew she would need to read in order to write the book he had in mind. He was grooming her to help him write the novel that turned out to be "Gone with the Wind".

On her twenty-fifth birthday, John brought home a table, and paper from his job, along with a used Remington typewriter and told her he was not going to bring any more books home for her to read, that she would have to write her own book.

Margaret was not a good typist therefore; she knew what he wanted her to do would not be easy, in fact, she thought it was impossible. Her typing skills had not improved since she worked at the Journal.

She asked him what he wanted her to write about, and he said "write about what you know best" which of course was her own life experiences, along with the stories she had heard from her elderly relatives who were veterans of the civil war and had lived through the battle of Atlanta.

During the time, she worked at the Atlanta journal John had taught her enough about typing that she could get by with his help. When she started to write the book she was so excited that she would be up, and typing when her housekeeper Bessie came to work in the morning at 7: am.

As long as she was excited over her subjects, and what she was writing about she had no problem writing. He had done a superb job of manipulation to get her to write what he wanted her to write, and to think it was her idea.

At night when he came home from work he would try to build up her confidence by telling her how talented he thought she was, and what a wonderful job she was doing.

That worked for him at first however, he was dealing with someone who had no self-discipline, and whose attention span, and outlook on life was completely different from his, a woman who quickly became bored.

It was at those times when she was under stress that she would come down with some kind of exotic illness, and have to go to the doctor. She was always complaining with some ailment or sprain, or broken bone, some of them she would have to go to a specialist that could not come up with a diagnosis, and that John couldn't afford.

He confided in his brother Gordon once while he and his wife were visiting them that he thought many of her illnesses were just in her mind, although some of them lasted for months, and sometimes for years, depending on what she was involved in at the time that she didn't want to do.

She took each member of her family, and played with the truth, making each of them more exciting than they had ever been by mixing their personalities up enough that if they were to ever read what she had written about them that they would never recognize themselves.

The only two family members she worried about causing her any problem about the characters in the book were her grandmother, and her ex-husband Red Berrien Upshaw. They were the only ones she thought would recognize themselves in the book that could, or would cause her trouble.

Although John was at work during the day, she knew she would have to deal with his disappointment if she didn't complete the assignment he had given her the night before that she had to complete every day. This went on from 1926 until 1930 when she quit working on the book, and John took over.

When he was at home, they were always involved in something to do with the book. His desire to write the great American novel and her desire to get revenge on Atlanta society for their failure to accept her membership in the Junior League years before was a driving force for her.

She never thought about the book in the same way John did. Actually, it was not much more than garbage in her mind. John kept trying to convince her it was good, and they could get it published, but she didn't believe him.

He never gave up on it even when she would stop working on it for months at a time, making him show his disappointment in her. He had his own personal way to let her know when he was upset with her. And most of the time it was over the book.

After the first year of their marriage, they had very little social life, or outside interests that were not related to the research, writing, and editing of the book. How John kept, her focused enough to write the stories for four years is beyond my ability to comprehend.

Margaret didn't have a clear goal in mind for the book, but John did. He desperately wanted the book finished, and published, but he knew she would have to do the storytelling as she had done since starting it.

He had taught her a lot since they met however, with her lack of education, and bad grammar she couldn't have completed the book without his immeasurable contribution, and perseverance.

She didn't have the technical skills, the self-discipline or the confidence to turn her ideas into a completed manuscript of the quality of "Gone with the Wind". The insecurity she felt hampered her in many ways making her easily manipulated by John.

To make matters worse she was spoiled, and demanding and John was in a different category altogether. He was willing to do whatever it took to get her to write the stories about her family the civil war, and the battle of Atlanta, and his sacrifice was greater than anyone could have imagined.

She was never as excited, or as fascinated by the book as John was. She knew her limitations, and she knew she didn't have what it would take to write anything then get it published on her own, that had been proven to her repeatedly when she presented her work to publishers and received a rejection.

He knew that together they could accomplish his goal however; they would have to live without outside interference. They would both have to contribute he would work, and he expected her to spend her days writing the stories then after they had dinner he would edit, and re-write what she had written that day, and that definately wasn't the lifestyle she wanted. She hated the isolation and the fact that she no longer had friends dropping in because she had made a "bargain" with John that he made her honor.

I found it interesting that shortly after Red Upshaw had been in Atlanta in 1927, John spent three weeks in the hospital with one of his psychosomatic illnesses, where his doctors couldn't find anything wrong with him; he was back at work in two weeks after his release from the hospital. The cause of his illness was never established.

This was a pattern for him and for Margaret when they were experiencing personal stressful situations. I question why a visit from Upshaw to Atlanta would have such a negative effect on John especially when there was no evidence that he contacted them while he was in town.

After the crisis passed Margaret went back to work on the book, until the summer of 1928, when she quit working on it again. John was upset with her for what he called her lack of self-confidence. I think it was just her way of objecting to his altering, and taking apart, what she was writing.

He refused to accept any responsibility for her actions when she would put her work away for what would sometimes be several month's. After he had aggressively edited and altered what she had written.

Margaret was not the kind of woman who wouldn't be offended if he constantly criticized her work, and especially when he was changing it to something, she didn't recognize as something she wrote, and that was happening often in the latter stages of the book.

In November 1928, one of her distant cousins died, and she attended the funeral, when she returned home she realized the funeral had generated in her mind a new chapter that was one of many instances where she used family events in her stories.

Margaret stopped working on it again in 1929, and John soon realized there was no way he could convince her she was wrong to put it away again, that she needed to finish it. His only option was to help her find a place to store the envelopes containing all of the chapters until he could convince her to continue with it.

The last thing in the world John wanted was for her to quit working on the book, but he couldn't force her to continue. When she had been away from it for several months, he had never let her forget it was unfinished, and that she was not keeping her end of the "bargain".

He accused her of being ungrateful for her god given ability to write. She was not at all impressed with his obsession with the book, and she definitely wasn't concerned with the fact that he had promised her that he would make her rich, and famous, she didn't believe that for a minute.

He saw what he was doing as being helpful and necessary. I think she saw it as criticism when he severely edited her stories, and changed them until she couldn't recognize them as something she had written.

It looked as though she was not going to finish it at least any time soon. It had become such an overwhelming job for her that she felt she just couldn't continue with it. The possibility of not finishing it didn't disturb Margaret, because she was never convinced of its potential to be successful anyway.

John was in charge of everything he knew what they had, and he was furious with her because he couldn't convince her to complete it. That was when he decided that he was going to have to do something to energize her interest in finishing it.

In 1930, he got a promotion to Advertising Manager of Georgia Power; with the additional money the promotion afforded him, he could buy a car although he didn't drive apparently because of his occasional epileptic seizures. Margaret always drove them where they wanted to go.

The car gave John the opportunity to renew her interest, in the book by taking her on Sunday outings to various Civil War battle-fields in, and around Atlanta that made her happy, and relaxed where she would recall stories she had heard, that was easy for her to include in the stories she had written for the book.

Margaret had always said she was writing the book just for their amusement, and she was never as excited as John was about it. He just had to keep her on track until she finished the artistic part of it, then his job would begin. His work on the book after Macmillan, returned it, in addition to his full time job at the Georgia Power Company would just about kill him.

John received a small pay raise in 1932, and by then he had almost paid all of their huge doctor, and hospital bills along with other debts they had. He felt finally they could afford to move. They found a larger five-room apartment, at Two East Seventeenth Street. After the move, she got enough Victorian Furniture from her Grandmother Stephens to furnish her new apartment.

From 1930 to 1935, Margaret worked on the book very little, John had taken over, and he was working on it every night regardless of his demanding work schedule.

The convenient problem she was complaining about at that time was her eyes that prevented her from writing, or anything to do with the book. She could always use illness or some kind of injury to put the book away when she didn't want to work on it.

His favorite place to work on it was on their sun porch with the windows open where they had set up an office. That was where he worked to figure out an opening chapter for the book. It was a place where he could relax, and be at peace away from her.

When he was trying to figure out how other writers started their novels he read, and studied the first chapter in numerous books to get an idea of how it works.

If he hadn't helped her write the book, he wouldn't have been the one trying to figure out how to start the opening chapter that would have been a job done by the author.

He kept trudging along until he had the manuscript where he wanted it to be. I cannot imagine what he had to deal with to produce the finished product. Just as her brother Stephens Mitchell said, he had to take what she wrote, and change what he didn't like about it.

In 1935, Harold Latham from Macmillan Publishing was on a recruiting trip in the south, especially to Atlanta looking for new authors, and manuscripts. Lois Cole who was an employee of Macmillan's Atlanta office, had met Margaret at a social event, and learned that she was writing a civil war novel, and had told Latham about her.

Lois contacted Margaret, and told her when Latham would be in Atlanta, and asked her to set up a luncheon with some of the local authors. When Latham asked her about her own book, she told him she didn't have one.

Afterward when she was taking some of the young author's home, one of them confronted her about why Latham had asked her about her book. She laughingly made a joke about how funny it was that anyone would believe she could be an author and her comments made Margaret furious, it caused her to go home and get the manuscript that wasn't ready to be published, and take it to the hotel where Latham was getting ready to leave.

As soon as John found out, she had given Macmillan the unfinished manuscript she called them immediately, and ask that they return it. I question whether he made her ask for the manuscript back or if it was her idea. I doubt that she was knowledgeable enough to know that it was not ready for publishing, or how much work it would take to complete it.

It became obvious to Macmillan soon after they returned the book to Margaret that John was in control of it. Afterwards their communication was mostly with him. They exchanged letters where he was answering their questions, and telling them the progress he was making.

There is no way that Macmillan didn't understand that John Marsh was the brains behind Gone with the Wind, and that he was totally in charge of it. He was the one who refused to let Macmillan editors edit it. They soon realized who they were dealing with, and although he went along with saying she was the author "he alone was in charge of completing the book".

Margaret Mitchell was never involved in legal affairs without input from either her father, or her brother, and you have to ask yourself would she have given the manuscript to Macmillan or to any other publisher without knowing the legal implications of her actions.

Both Margaret and John told people she was writing a book about the civil war. Neither of them ever said "they" were writing a book however, everyone knew his input was much more than editing and correcting grammar.

I wonder if anyone was advising her on the legal aspects of it, as well as what she would need to do to make sure she legally owned it. There is no way anyone will ever know if she was legally perceptive enough to figure it out for herself. It is obvious that someone with her educational background would not know whether the book was ready to give to a publisher.

I cannot imagine a situation where a man with John's education and intelligence, with a lifelong desire to be a famous writer would allow her to take the book from him without serious consequences.

Once her name went on the contract, he had no choice but to accept her actions. To question or to claim he co-wrote the book would have stirred up legal questions, and problems that could have caused Macmillan to withdraw their offer.

Margaret Mitchell was a woman who prior to giving the manuscript of "Gone With The Wind to Macmillan was devastated over the fact that everything she had ever sent to a publisher had been rejected, and John would let her know in his own way that he didn't like it when she did things he didn't approve of with the book.

After learning what Macmillan's reaction to the manuscript had been, John's excitement over the book escalated making him feel vindicated for his manipulation of Margaret to get it written.

After all, of the work, he had put into it, and the stress of trying to keep her focused on writing the stories he felt relieved that it was finally coming to completion, and he was willing to spend much more time on it to get it ready for publication.

John had worked on it for months until he made himself sick before the book was published and he had to be hospitalized. While he was in the hospital she put her maiden name on the book as the author giving her full credit.

Lois Cole from Macmillan wrote her a letter and said they needed to know if she wanted to sign the book Margaret Marsh, she replied with the following without an explanation, "Gone with the Wind by Margaret Mitchell."

First, she gave the manuscript to the representative from Macmillan, while John was at work, then while he was in the hospital she put her maiden name on it as the author. After all, of the work and stress he went through trying to get it finished by the deadline, she didn't have enough respect for him to use her married name as the author of the book.

By using her maiden name as the author there was nothing anywhere that connected the Marsh name to the book, destroying his lifelong dream of becoming a famous author. His plan to use her to become famous had backfired on him; he had made her rich and famous instead.

Before the contract was signed for the movie rights to Gone with the Wind Margaret was in North Carolina with friends while she corresponded by mail, and telegraph with John who was at home in Atlanta.

Spending months in North Carolina with her new friends seems a strange thing for her to do. I question whether she was with her ex-husband when she was suposedly visiting friends in North Carolina, That scenario was completely out of character for her.

John explained to her that he and her brother Stephens were taking care of everything, and that they didn't need her to be there. However, she telegraphed him "not to make any decisions without her" she told him not to do anything about the movie rights that she would take care of it when she returned home.

This was her way of telling John that she was in control of the "Gone with the Wind" business. That she would handle it even though he had almost died from overwork with very little rest, while he worked a full time job, then going home and working on the book until the wee hours of the morning for years.

Prior to the deal with Selznick on the making of a movie from the book, was the first visible sign of her usurping her authority making it obvious there was serious trouble between her and John? After the book was on the market, and they had money coming it's possible she thought she didn't need him any longer.

She came home from her stay in North Carolina to get ready to go to New York with her brother Stephens to sign the contract for the movie rights. John didn't go to New York with them, and wasn't included in those final negotiations. That had to have some kind of negative impact on him.

She didn't come back to Atlanta from New York with her brother; instead, she went back to North Carolina, where her friends were, she was acting as though she had no obligation to Atlanta, or to John Marsh.

Shortly thereafter, she started having a serious problem with her eyes, and had to return home to Atlanta to take care of that problem. When she arrived in Atlanta on the train, John met her at the station on his way to Kentucky.

He knew what her problem was, and that she could barely see, but he didn't postpone his trip, he left her to take care of her eye problem on her own, while he continued on his trip not letting her blindness interfere with his plans.

This was unusual behavior for John, He had always been attentive to her needs however; this time he refused to be deterred by her whatever her problem was whether it was her eyes, or some other melodramatic illness, and he continued on his way.

He probably thought the blindness was another of her unexplainable illnesses brought on by whatever was happening to her at the moment. I think when he returned from Kentucky was when he put a stop to whatever she had been up to in North Carolina, and he never let up on her afterwards until she died.

Writing all of those hundreds of thank you letters to author's and other knowledgeable people who had praised her literary expertise for writing "Gone with the Wind" giving her full credit for it must have caused extreme shame, and turmoil in her mind. She knew it was not her literary expertise, and knowledge they were praising it was "John's".

She had to know that the newspaper people who were her friends and people who had known her all of her life knew she didn't have what it took to write a book of the importance of "Gone With the Wind". Everyone who knew them knew that without John Marsh she had never been successful at anything.

A friend of both Margaret and John was Ralph McGill a newspaperman from the Atlanta Constitution commenting on the ability of Margaret to write "Gone With the Wind" he said for her to write that book she would have had to have a genie, but she didn't need a genie because she had John Marsh.

What McGill was actually saying was that it was virtually impossible with her lack of education, and literary experience to write a book of that importance, and magnitude without the tremendous help, and know how of John Marsh.

She lived in fear from the time the book was available to the public, until her death, that someone would legally challenge the authorship of it, and on whose life she had based the characters, especially the character of Rhett Butler. She was well aware that Red Upshaw would see himself in that character in her book.

If she had been the sole author of the book, and she had not used people she knew or family member's as character's in the book, she wouldn't have been so worried about public scrutiny.

The most gratification she ever received from it was the fact that she went from being a social disgrace in Atlanta, to being their icon. Deep down she knew that the fame she achieved from the book didn't belong just to her, that it also belonged to her husband John Marsh; after all, he worked on it as much, if not more than, she did from 1926, until 1936 when it was published.

In late 1948, nine months before her death Margaret changed her will. Later she called her brother into conference on several nights to discuss organizing her affairs. She had already made her will, therefore; why would she need his assistance for several days, with no mention of John.

After many conversations, on numerous subjects Stephens brought up religion, and she replied that she didn't want to talk about that, because she hadn't been involved with the Catholic Church for many years.

This so-called conference with her brother took several days. There was no mention of where John was during that time. I have to wonder if what took place during that meeting could have been the trigger that led to her death. The will probated after her death was the hand written one she made in 1948, not one her brother drafted.

She said when you make a "bargain with a devil" you had better stick to your bargain. I may have made one, but whenever I give my word on something, or whenever I take a course of action, I am not going to try to crawl out of that course of action, because I may have made a mistake in starting it. It is not the fair thing to do.

Was she referring to the bargain she made with John Marsh when they agreed to get married to write a book, and he promised to make her rich and famous, or was she referring to her husband who in her mind had turned into a devil that was making her life a living hell?

John told Medora Perkerson the wife of the editor of the Atlanta Journal after Margaret's death in 1949, that he was actively involved with her every step of the way from the beginning to the end.

He didn't explain why he never received any recognition other than the dedication she had insisted the publisher insert in the book. Neither did she question him about why Margaret failed to share the authorship of the book with him.

At first, she accepted the praise, and glory that went along with being the author of a best selling novel however; after a while, it began to sink in that she had taken credit for John's work, and everyone knew it.

That was a hard pill for her to swallow, because her father had pounded into her that you don't take credit for the work of others, only Margaret didn't posess her father's ethical standard.

When the many rumors and the suspicion about her ability to write a book of the quality, and magnitude of "Gone with the Wind" surfaced, she became so paranoid that most of her time was spent denying, and trying to quiet the rumors.

She was never successful in convincing people who knew her educational background, and lifestyle that she alone wrote the big book. There were rumors that John had written it, but she denied he ever did anything more than edit.

According to her brother Stephens Mitchell the most persistent rumor was that Margaret had not written it at all, he explained that many people claimed John Marsh wrote it.

He went on to say that, she wrote most of the story, and John edited, and changed what he didn't like about it. In other words, Stephens Mitchell admitted that his sister "was not the sole author of "Gone with the Wind".

Stephens knew his sister didn't write the book without John Marsh helping her every step of the way, reading and changing what she wrote to make it readable, and publishable. He knew she couldn't write anything without profanity, bad grammar, and misspelled words

I have never understood why her brother didn't question the bizarre circumstances of her death, especially after the strange way she had been acting since 1944 right up until she died. There were many signs of trouble that should have thrown up red flags that everything was not what it seemed.

I also question why John left Stephens Mitchell the rights to "Gone With the Wind" in his will instead of leaving it to be shared equally with his family, who were as deserving as her brother was from the work John had done to make the book possible.

Prior to their death their lifestyle changed very little they lived in the same frugal way they had lived during the depression when John was working at the Georgia Power Company there is no way they could have spent the millions generated from "Gone With The Wind" before their death

JOHN MARSH RETIRED

O ther situations kept arising that delayed any action John could have taken to remedy his unacceptable home life, such as the foreign rights to the book that took John and Stephens Mitchell ten more years to straighten out.

Although they no longer needed his salary from the power company, he continued to work keeping himself too busy to think about his living situation after all it kept him away from her during the day.

In the fall of 1947, when her husband retired from the Georgia Power Company something was happening with Margaret that she didn't discuss with anyone.

Her secretary said she was acting differently than she had ever seen her act, she said she became careless about her grooming habits, and she was irritable all of the time

The most unexpected thing she did was to cancel their listing in the Atlanta Telephone Directory, her brother found this to be strange since her popularity from the book was no longer a problem, and she hadn't changed it when she was being overwhelmed with unwanted calls.

Stephens Mitchell said his sister had become tired, nervous, and irritable, and whatever was bothering her was beginning to show, she began to look older, and a strained look had come into her face, he said he had never known her to be like this in her life.

It was then that she began drinking more, she had started getting champagne cocktails delivered to her apartment from the driving club across the street on a daily basis, and that could account for some of her unusual behavior.

Margaret was reportedly going through the worst spell of depression that she had ever experienced, and the drinking certainly would have contributed to it. If someone was threatening her life, she may have feared her death was imminent.

In November 1948, Margaret changed her will, in January 1949 Red Upshaw reportedly committed suicide, and Margaret Mitchell died in August 1949. All in a nine month span of time.

In September 1947 after his second heart attack, John Marsh resigned from the Georgia Power Company, and was confined to the apartment that was not a pleasant experience for him.

Thereafter living in the apartment with Margaret, who was someone he could deal with as long as he was working, and out of the home during the day., but now he had no place to go to get away from her.

Working on the book related issues until late at night kept his mind occupied allowing him to close her, and all of her aches and pains, of which she complained incessantly out of his mind temporarily.

The stress of the book took a physical claim on John it took away all of his ambitions, and dreams as well. Retirement would mean confinement with Margaret, and as he told his mother close confinement with a woman was not acceptable to him, as a result he had kept his job until he had to retire due to stress, after his second heart attack.

John Marsh led the police, and the court that tried my dad to believe that he was physically impaired to the degree that he needed help to walk on level ground.

If that were true, how did he manage to climb up and down thirty steps every time he left their apartment to go across the street to the Driving Club to have drinks with his friends every day, as Margaret said, he had started doing after his retirement.

It takes someone who can run, and move quickly to jaywalk on busy four lane city streets. If he were as physically impaired as he wanted everyone to believe how could he jaywalk in Atlanta's busy streets weaving in and out of traffic as their friends said he and his wife had a habit of doing.

Was he checking out how easy it would be to push his wife in front of a moving car? Murder by vehicle that would look like an accident is what my dad said happened to Margaret Mitchell.

John's doctor told him he should never go back to his job at the Power Company, where he would have to work under stress. However, he recommended daily exercise.

His doctor knew he was not an invalid that couldn't walk without help. The fact that he told his mother he didn't take any medication tells me he was in pretty darn good health.

Being an invalid was how he kept anyone from believing he was strong enough to shove his wife under a moving car. I don't buy that scenario for a second.

He told his mother in September 1947 after he had resigned from the Georgia Power Company that his doctor had prescribed a drink of whiskey in the afternoon. He said another medicine I take now and then is namely a "Hershey bar" he told her he didn't have any pain or discomfort of any kind except that it was annoying to tire so quickly.

In his own words, he told his mother he was not an invalid, however, that is not what he wanted the police, the court and the media to believe. He had a heart problem that was serious, but he was not the invalid he pretended to be.

Their secretary Margaret Baugh said John had recovered from his heart attack, and that Margaret should have been happy but she wasn't. I don't understand why no one tried to find out why she wasn't happy that her husbands health had improved, and she no longer had to worry about money.

They were both as miserably unhappy as two people could possibly be. They no longer had anything to talk about since she took ownership of the book, and had put her maiden name on it as the author, destroying his dream of being a famous author.

After the book was finished, and she cut him out of any participation in the negotiations for the movie rights, their life together took on new meaning after that. It was the end for her. Now they found themselves stuck with each other, and there is no way it could have been a pleasant experience for either of them.

After twenty-four years of living with a woman whose personality and everything about her clashed with who he was, and how he wanted to live had to be less than a pleasant experience for him.

Having to live with a man who was so extremely different from her caused her to become severely depressed, and unhappy. Before she met John She told her pen pal Allen Edee that she "couldn't love", and that she would never marry.

Then John Marsh changed her mind and talked her into what many people thought was a platonic relationship to write a book that was successful, and made her rich, but it didn't make either of them happy.

In the fall of 1948, news of Red Upshaw came to their attention again after years of silence, and I find it strange that just a short time after Upshaw was trying to contact Margaret that she would make a new will, and two months later he would commit suicide.

I wonder if it was really a suicide or did something; more sinister possibly happen to him? Whether or not Red Upshaw inquiring about her had anything to do with her decision to change her will is unknown.

In January 1949, seven months before her own death, Margaret received a newspaper clipping from the Galveston Texas Daily News from her ex-husbands stepmother that Berrien Kinnard Upshaw died from a fall from the fifth floor of a downtown hotel.

His death had been ruled a suicide. Her only reaction to his death was to say to her secretary Margaret Baugh "what a horrible way to die". I believe she had a strong connection to Red Upshaw that she could never overcome,

I think it was an attraction to his wild side that excited her I don't believe it was love. It was her rebellion for something forbidden. I think she was incapable of real love.

I haven't been able to determine where John was at that time except their secretary said she would have preferred to tell him about Upshaw's death first, and let him tell Margaret, but he was unavailable. What John said when he learned of Red Upshaw's aleged suicide is unknown to me.

In the late Summer of 1987, on a trip to Atlanta, Marianne Walker who was doing research for her book on Margaret Mitchell and John Marsh had a meeting with Deon Rutledge the daughter of Bessie Jordan who was the Marsh long time housekeeper, and maid.

Deon had practically grown up in the Marsh apartment, and she was well aware of everything that took place there. As an adult, she temporarily took over the duties of her mother for a short time in the Marsh household, while her mother was ill, and couldn't work.

She was fond of both Margaret and John although it was obvious to her that they had very different personalities. As the meeting was ending, Walker said Deon looked up and made the statement that "folks don't know it, but he helped her write that book".

That statement from Deon Rutledge who had first hand knowledge of the authorship of the book, spoke the truth that Margaret Mitchell would never admit.

John Marsh did help her write the book just like Deon said, and Margaret never admitted to anyone that he did anything more than edit, and correct grammar which is absurdly ridiculous to anyone who has taken the time to read about her lack of education, her background, and history.

In the years, he lived with Margaret Mitchell, and they were working on the book he was learning from her as much as she was learning from him. He had heard all of her stories from her childhood therefore; when he took over to finish writing the book in the early 1930s, he could easily finish it from where she left off.

Margaret Mitchell was perfectly qualified to write short stories about the Civil War and its aftermath, she was not educationally qualified to complete a novel of the magnitude, and quality of "Gone with the Wind" without the dedicated help of John Marsh.

METAPHOR'S FOR
MURDER

According to Marianne Walker in Margaret Mitchell & John Marsh The Love Story Behind Gone With The Wind John wrote metaphors to his family and to his friend Sue Myrick that I refer to here as his metaphor's for murder.

He wrote to his family in 1949 before Margaret's death, that if a person is in pain it doesn't matter whether the pain comes from a broken leg, or from cracker crumbs in the bed, maybe there is nothing you can do about the broken leg, but you can brush out the cracker crumbs, and if the sum total of the pain is reduced the sick person is better off.

When John Marsh who thought of himself as an invalid who was in pain caused by his wife, shoved Margaret Mitchell in front of my dad's car he was physically brushing the cracker crumbs out of his bed.

He realized he couldn't do anything about his heart problem, but he would be better off with her gone, then he could live the remainder of his life in peace without having to share his life with her, or any woman.

November 27, 1950, almost a year after Margaret's death John wrote his friend Sue Myrick. The advantages of a sudden death have grown on me in these years when I have had much time for meditation. Some people can stand life with a ball and chain on their leg, just as some birds can survive with a broken wing, and some animals can endure life in a circus cage that is not a life I would have wished.

What he was saying was that the advantages of his wife's sudden death removed the ball and chain from around his leg and released him from living like an animal in a cage with Margaret. If that was the way, he saw his life with her, it could explain why he decided to kill her to remedy his situation.

He knew that he wouldn't live to old age with his heart problem, and he also knew that he didn't want to spend his last days with her making it imperative to find a way to remove her from his presence. Twenty-four years was all he could stand of her, and all of her aches and pains.

When he quoted the metaphor to Sue Myrick, he was trying to justify his actions in his own mind, that the end justifies the means.

It's very hard for me to imagine how someone can function without empathy.

When he retired, and had to live with a woman who was without a doubt not someone with whom he wanted to spend his last days on this earth, hence, he brushed the cracker crumbs out of his bed, and lived the remainder of his life in peace, instead of like an animal in a cage with her.

An emotional attachment to another person was something Margaret Mitchell and John Marsh knew they didn't possess. The only attactment she had for John was from the physical need for someone to rescue her from living in her family home under her father's rule and take care of her.

John needed to use her knowledge of the old south, and her story telling talent to become the famous writer he wanted to be unfortunately he would never get the credit he felt he deserved for his participation in the writing of the big book.

As far as the public worldwide was concerned she was the author of "Gone with the Wind" and the money was all that was left. The money could not make either of them happy and content. The book they sacrificed everything for ended up destroying them.

Before Christmas after his wife died on August 16, 1949, John bought a house and moved out of the apartment he had shared with Margaret. He lived in peace without having to live like an animal in a cage with a woman until he died from a heart attack the first week of May 1952.

When John Marsh died, he left all of the rights to "Gone with the Wind" to Stephens Mitchell. He made no mention of all the money generated from the book or what happened to it. Anyone looking at their lifestyle would ever believe they had a dime. They were living the same frugal way when she died that they had lived during the depression, before the book exploded, and he was working at the power company.

Someone once said that fame is a kind of death. That was certainly true for Margaret Mitchell after fame erupted into her life she became more depressed than she had ever been.

Her fame was a kind of death for John Marsh also, it took a physical claim on him taking away all of his dreams and ambitions, and left him confined in an apartment alone with her in a situation he never wanted to find himself in.

When he was able to work and get out of the house every day he could handle the few hours he had to put up with her unusual personality and quirks.

When he retired and was confined with her he had to find a way to brush the cracker crumbs out of his bed, and get over the feeling that he was living like an animal in a cage, he knew he couldn't stand for very long.

That left him with no other alternative than to find a way to remove her from his life. Dad said the way he solved his problem was to get her intoxicated lead her out into traffic jaywalking on Peachtree Street, then he shoved her backwards into the path of his car.

Dad's Obituary

Obituary from Cumming Ga. [AP}

Man Who Killed Margaret Mitchell Dies

Hugh Dorsey Gravitt, the cab driver whose car struck and killed author Margaret Mitchell in 1949, has died at age 74.

Gravitt, of Covington died Friday, and a funeral was held at Ingram's Funeral Home in Cumming

In August 1949, the off-duty cab driver struck Miss Mitchell as she walked with her husband John Marsh, across Peachtree Street in downtown Atlanta.

Five days later, the 48 year old author of "Gone With The Wind" died.

Gravitt was convicted of involuntary Manslaughter and served about ten months in prison

In a 1991 interview, Gravitt said Miss Mitchell darted in front of his car and he tried to miss her but he couldn't He said the accident scarred him for life.

"I'd rather it had been me instead of her," he said. "It won't ever heal." Celestine Sibley an Atlanta Journal Constitution columnist who covered Miss Mitchell[s funeral, said many people blamed Gravitt because of a photo of Gravitt taken during his fingerprinting, the photographer told him to smile, and he did.

She recalled. "He later said, I didn't feel like smiling...and I don't know why I did."

In addition to driving a cab, Gravitt worked as a mechanic, landscaper and service station operator.

MY DAD'S DEATH

T he day my dad died April 15, 1994, began as every day since I admitted him four days earlier to Our Lady of Perpetual Help Hospice in Atlanta Georgia with terminal lung cancer. They told me his time was short however; I didn't expect it to come so soon. When early in the morning I received a phone call from the hospice that I needed to get there as soon as I could.

As I showered, and got dressed then drove the thirty miles to Atlanta my thoughts were on what I was about to lose. My dad the person responsible for my existence, someone who could never be equaled or replaced in my life.

I had made a promise to him that I would never put him in a nursing home or a hospital of any kind as long as it was possible for me to take care of him at home.

Unfortunately the time came that he needed care I couldn't give him and putting him in that place to die was agonizingly painful for me. I spent weeks that I had trouble sleeping with the feeling I had let him down.

I had taken him home from the hospital two weeks earlier against the advice of his doctor who told me I wouldn't be able to take care of him at home however; I just couldn't do anything else without trying to take care of him myself first.

After I took him home, I soon learned that I had made a mistake. I wasn't able to sleep without restraining him where he couldn't get out of the bed. The week I kept him at home I was afraid to go sound asleep afraid he would get up and go outside, or fall.

I thought about how after a week of struggling to try to keep him at home with me it wasn't working. The cancer was taking its toll. I soon realized he wasn't going to survive and that what I was trying to do was not helping him, therefore I had to do something else.

I called an ambulance, and took him back to the hospital, where shortly thereafter he was transferred to the hospice. I was so distraught over the fact that I was going to lose my dad who had become such a part of my life, and that I would miss him more than anything I could find words to describe.

I thought about the past three years that I had spent taking care of him; the things we talked laughed, and cried about. I thought about all the hurt and anguish he had suffered during his lifetime, and how happiness and peace of mind always seemed to elude him.

I thought about how hard he had to work to survive, with very little compensation, or appreciation.

Then I thought about Margaret Mitchell's death, and his conviction for involuntary manslaughter that imprisoned him in protective custody for almost a year. I thought about the secret he had kept for four decades before he told me what had actually happened to her and afterward how relieved he was to share the burden he had carried for so long.

I thought about how I was going to keep his funeral from becoming a media circus by the people who had tortured him for those forty-five years without even knowing what the truth was about Margaret Mitchell's death.

When I arrived at the hospice, and went to dad's room a nun was there, and she told me a priest wanted to talk to me. As soon as I looked at dad, I knew he was dying. At that moment I felt a deep sadness, and more alone than I had ever felt in my life.

A short time later a priest came into the room, and asked me about dad's religious background. I had never discussed religion with him enough that I would know for sure; I had always just assumed his religious beliefs were personal to him as mine are to me. The only thing I knew for sure was that he was not Catholic.

I know he believed in god and prayed. He told me about what he did at the scene of the incident after he hit Margaret Mitchell as well as in the jail when he prayed for her to recover from her injuries. Praying to god to give him the strength to get through what he would be facing in the days to come.

My feeling when my dad was at deaths door was that it didn't matter what denomination his religious leanings were. I didn't know anything about the Catholic belief system and it wasn't important he was in a Catholic facility, and I felt blessed that a Priest was there, and with my permission, he read the last rites.

A few hours later, the pain, and grief my dad suffered for forty-five years ended quietly. When he died, I went through months of grieving, just as I did with my son, and my mother wondering if there was anything I could have done to prolong his life.

I knew I had done my best to make his last days as happy and good for him as I possibly could. The thing that bothered me the most about his death was that he could never tell the world how Margaret Mitchell died, and that he was not the person responsible for her death.

I thank God that I could spend the last three years of his life with him. It was a good for me to spend quality time with him, and I know it was a good for him also. When dad and I were talking, and re-living the past we were at peace.

It was something he had never had time for before. We talked about what he wanted me to do after his death, and he told me if I found it to be something I couldn't do for me not to worry about it, that he understood how hard it would be for me to confront the past with what he had told me. He was definately right about that,it has taken me twenty years to keep my promise to him.

We helped each other through a trying time in our life, both of us benefited from the time we could spend together, he was a pleasant person to live with, and I wish I could have had many more years with him. It just ended too soon.

My dad said John Marsh committed the perfect murder when he shoved his wife in front of his car, so perfect that he was never required to admit or deny it.

Dad said the evidence that would have exonerated him from the nightmare he had lived for all those years was there for anyone who cared enough about justice to look. No one in the sixty-two years since it happened has ever questioned the part John Marsh played in the death of his wife until now.

Margaret Mitchell never found the peace, and happiness that everyone strives for in life however; she didn't deserve to die in the violent way she did.

I hope she found the peace in death that she could never find in the troubled life she led. Most of her unhappiness was of her own making.

I believe she deserves for the truth to finally be told. Don't ever forget her warning that when you make a bargain with a devil you had better follow through.

Bibliography

1: Hugh Dorsey Gravitt -1991/1994.

2: Department of Public Safety- Accident Report with drawing August 11, 1949 Signed by Hugh Dorsey Gravitt.

3: Department of Public Safety Accident Report filed with Clerk of Fulton County Court August 24, 1949.

4: Georgia State Patrol-Motor-Vehicle Accident-Death-Statistical Transcript August 12, 1949.

5: Certificate of Death - Margaret Munnarlyn Mitchell Marsh- August 19, 1949.

6: Indictment- State of Georgia - Fulton County. August 23, 1949

7: Sentence Fulton Superior Court State of Georgia- November 16, 1949.

8: Upshaw Divorce-Fulton County Georgia- October 16, 1924.

9: Anne Edwards- Road To Tara - Ticknor & Fields, New Haven New York -Copyright 1983- ISBN-0-89919-89919-16g-x

10: Marianne Walker - Margaret Mitchell & John Marsh - The Love Story Behind Gone With the Wind - Peachtree Publishing, 494 Armour Circle N.E. Atlanta, Georgia 30324 - Copyright 1993 - ISBN-1-56145-082-0

11: Darden Asbury Pyron - Southern Daughter - Oxford University Press- Copyright 1991- ISBN-0-19-505276-5

12: A Dynamo Going To Waste-Peachtree Publishing-Copyright 1985- Library of Congress Catalog # 85-60337- ISBN-0931948-70-3.

13: Atlanta Journal Newspaper- Microfilm - August 12, 1949 Margaret Mitchell Marsh Lies On Peachtree Street After Being Struck By Car.

14: Atlanta Journal Newspaper - Microfilm- August 12, 1949 - Margaret Mitchell Continues In Coma By Robert H. McKee.

15: Atlanta Journal Newspaper- Microfilm - August 12, 1949 - Remorseful Driver Prays For Peggy by Orville Gaines

16: Atlanta Journal Newspaper - Microfilm - Tuesday Evening August 16, 1949 - Margaret Mitchell Dies after Five Day Battle, By William Key.

17: Atlanta Constitution Newspaper - Microfilm - August 18, 1949 - Jaywalkers Liable Under Judges Rule.

18: Atlanta Journal Newspaper- Microfilm - Tuesday Evening August 16, 1949- Jenkins To Ask Murder Bill Against Driver.

19: Atlanta Constitution Newspaper - Microfilm - August 17, 1949 - Gravitt Held On Charge Of Murder By Keeler McCartney.

20: Atlanta Constitution Newspaper - Microfilm- August 18, 1949 - Truman Wire Comforts Marsh after Margaret Mitchell's Death.

21: Atlanta Journal Newspaper - Microfilm - Traffic Court Hearing for Gravitt Set for August 24, 1949.

22: Atlanta Journal Newspaper - Microfilm - August 25, 1949 Driver Cleared, Pedestrians Fined in Accident here.

23: Atlanta Constitution newspaper - Microfilm - August 1949 - Crackdown on Cab drivers.

24: Atlanta Journal Newspaper - Microfilm - Tuesday Evening November 15, 1949 40-To Ask Murder Bill against Driver..

25: 50 MPH Speed Claimed for Mitchell Death Car, Gravitt Goes On Trial On Manslaughter Charge by Margaret Shannon.

26: Atlanta Journal Newspaper - Microfilm - November 16, 1949 - "Unavoidable" Gravitt's Plea by Margaret Shannon.

27: Atlanta Journal Newspaper - Microfilm - November 17, 1949 - Gravitt Is Given 12-18 Months in Mitchell Death by Marjory Smith.

28: Atlanta Journal Newspaper - Microfilm - August 25, 1949 - Arnold Binds Gravitt on Traffic Counts.

29: Atlanta Constitution Newspaper - Microfilm - August 17, 1949 - Gravitt "Good Driver" Taxi Official Declares.

30: Wrongs and Rights Louis Roney. http://www.golfest.com/Events/Asp?ID=3

31: Psychiatrist Hervey Cleckley- The Mask of Sanity ISBN 0-9621519

32: Without Consecience by Robert D. Hare. http://www.hare.org/welcome/bio.html